∞

Holy Simplicity

Raoul Plus, S.J.

Holy Simplicity

SOPHIA INSTITUTE PRESS®
Manchester, New Hampshire

Holy Simplicity was originally published under the title *Simplicity* by The Newman Press, Westminster, Maryland, in 1951. Chapter 1 from the original edition has been omitted from this 2009 edition by Sophia Institute Press®, and minor editorial revisions have been made.

Sophia Institute Press®
Box 5284, Manchester, NH 03108
1-800-888-9344
www.sophiainstitute.com

Nihil obstat: Patricius Morris, S.T.D., L.S.S., *Censor Deputatus*
Imprimatur: E. Morrogh Bernard, *Vicarius Generalis*
Westminster, November 15, 1949

Library of Congress Cataloging-in-Publication Data

Plus, Raoul, 1882-1958.
   [Simplicité. English]
   Holy simplicity / Raoul Plus.
     p. cm.
   Originally published: Simplicity. Westminster, Md. :
   Newman Press, 1951.
   Includes bibliographical references.
   ISBN 978-1-933184-51-7 (pbk. : alk. paper) 1. Simplicity
   — Religious aspects — Christianity. I. Title.
   BV4647.S48P55813 2009
   241'.4 — dc22

                            2009012169

09 10 11 12 13 14 9 8 7 6 5 4 3 2 1

Contents

∞

Editor's note: The biblical quotations in the following pages are taken from the Douay-Rheims edition of the Old and New Testaments. Where applicable, quotations have been cross-referenced with the differing names and enumeration in the Revised Standard Version, using the following symbol: (RSV =).

∞

Holy Simplicity

Chapter 1

∽

The Simple Soul Focuses on God

To his priests on the mission, St. Vincent de Paul[1] explained, "There are two kinds of simplicity — one purely natural and silly found in people without judgment or discernment; a simplicity that is worth nothing, or at least is not a virtue. There is another simplicity that comprises the essential rightness of keeping our words and thoughts clear of all deceit and complexity, and makes us go straight to God and our neighbor without evasion or pretense."[2]

We must define what simplicity is as a virtue. The term can have two meanings. It may bear a general meaning that is abstract and theoretical, the total absence of duality, of any compounding of elements; or it can be given a more restricted and concrete sense, corresponding rather more closely to the common interpretation. In the first case, we are concerned rather with metaphysics; in the second, the perspective is more psychological.

To make both points of view clearer, we need only ponder in the first case what philosophy and theology tell us of the existence

---

[1] St. Vincent de Paul (1580-1660), founder of the Lazarist Fathers and the Sisters of Charity.

[2] Louis Déplanque, *Saint Vincent de Paul sous l'emprise chrétienne* (Bloud and Gay), 266.

and nature of God; and in the second, what we learn from the habitual behavior of little children. We will consider these two aspects separately for our enlightenment; but we must not be surprised if in practice they become merged together, enriching and completing each other.

∞

God has multiple attributes: goodness, wisdom, knowledge, and so on. It is more accurate to say, not that God *has* wisdom, goodness, knowledge, but that God *is* goodness, wisdom, knowledge. All His perfections blend into one unity. In Him — as one author expresses it — "Simplicity is the root of infinity."[3] Therefore, we can understand why Bossuet and St. Vincent de Paul exhort us to meditate on the unique simplicity of God, to help us to practice this virtue of virtues on our own level.

No other virtue, declares St. Vincent de Paul, serves better to draw us close to God. "It makes us like unto Him insofar as He is a sole being, one and uncompounded. We must strive to become in virtue what God is in nature."[4] Bossuet, trying to inspire the court

---

[3] Grou, *Manual for Interior Souls*. Another Jesuit, Father Nieremberg, says similarly, "Amongst the divine attributes there is not only an outward unity, but a very real one — an absolute identity. In God His merciful goodness and His stern justice, His immensity and indivisibility, His awful majesty and His loving kindness are all only one and the same thing. There is no distinction between His power and His wisdom, between His wisdom and His justice, His justice and His goodness, His goodness and His providence, or between that providence and His infinity. How wonderful it is to behold every perfection united in the simplicity of His nature" (*La Beauté de Dieu* [Vroment, Brussels, 1902], 61).

[4] St. Vincent de Paul, *Elévations, prières, et pensées* (de Gigord), 110-114.

circle with disgust for the complications of an intriguing and worldly life, showed them how God held all such things at naught. "Our vain pomps and our artificial grandeur cannot arouse the slightest desire in Him whose immensity by its very nature contains everything."

Someone may say: I can understand that God is single, absolute; but at the Creation, did not He Himself establish a duality? Thenceforth there would be God and what He had made.

No. The Creation in no way lessens the perfect simplicity of God. His creatures will not be what they are if the constant support of the Most High does not maintain them in their existence as creatures; lacking that, they must immediately return to nothingness, and the prophet says with truth that in reality they are as naught before Him. The Creation is only the evidence, the proof by His actions of God's omnipresence and His ineffable immensity.

In bestowing existence, God still sought in all things His own glory; and man, the core of creation, had no other purpose, and still has no other reason for existing save to offer up to the Lord — Himself a person who can think and love — the homage of all living things. *Benedicite omnia opera Domini Domino.*

God alone: nothing in the eternal simplicity of God is changed. Not that the creature *is* God, as Pantheism would have it; but because the created is solely for God in destiny as it is solely from God in its origin.

It was man who was to bring division into the world, disrupting the sacred and simple plan of divine providence. In his disobedience at the beginning of the world, he swerved aside from God's will, making a god of things created. (How prodigally, alas, he sets up idols for his worship!)

Christ must come and, representing in Himself all mankind, the whole creation, restore to that creation its original vocation to simplicity — the focusing of itself solely on God alone. That is the glorious doctrine of the Mystical Body of Christ: we, all, its members, making one only with Him, the Head; we, all, one only with the One in whom the Father is well pleased.[5]

But note this well; the simplicity that would have been effortless if man had remained faithful must henceforth be laborious and doomed to atavistic ills. In man, the Fall has provoked the revolt of his senses against his reason; and around man the revolt of creation against his domination, until then so peacefully assured — a tragic duality, and one often changing into violent conflict.

How different were the relations of Adam and Eve with God before and after the Fall! Before, they had no fear of God; afterward, when He called, they hid like children caught in wrongdoing. How different, too, were their relations with each other! Before, each saw in the other nothing but divinely created beauty; afterward, beset by desire, they blushed to see each other naked.

If only Eve had answered the Devil's tempting with the cry of simplicity — "It is forbidden!" — like a child who is asked, "Why will you not do that?" and answers, "Because Mamma does not wish it," without need for further reasoning or question.

So we understand what is the real essence of simplicity. It exists in God supremely; it existed, still splendid, in man as he came from the hands of God. Through sin, Adam and Eve, for whom until then the Almighty was all, paused upon another object and used it in rebellion. Their outlook was no longer simple; they were less upright of heart. They had compared a creature to their sole

---

[5] St. Paul further describes the final, definite victory of simplicity, when at the end of the world Christ will gather to Himself all those whom He had chosen in His infallible determination, and will be "all in all" and come to the "perfect age."

Master — worse still, they had preferred the creature. That was the tremendous and tragic duality.

"I feel two men in me."

Two? Many — a legion. Once, the untroubled simplicity of a life completely focused on its true center; now, the chaos and complexity of a life with many centers of attraction.

To be compounded is not in itself an evil; but if a being made up of several elements is to retain beauty and harmony, those elements must be drawn into a unity. It is the same as the various instruments in an orchestra under the conductor's baton; or like our two eyes: the fact that we have two eyes does not in any way lessen the simplicity of the visual act, as what each eye records is transmitted by nerves to the same center.

In man before the Fall, there were indeed a body and a soul; but they were joined to form a perfectly harmonious entity. Now in man the senses revolt against the spirit — duality, almost tearing him asunder.

It is only by strength of will that we shall attain unity; the beast in us must be tamed, the instincts disciplined. St. Ignatius of Loyola[6] has well said at the beginning of his *Spiritual Exercises*, "To order your life as you desire, you must know how to conquer yourself."

Our Lord knew well that despite our vocation to struggle for the regained simplicity of unity in Him, we frequently lose control of ourselves, and so risk breaking our links with Him and turning aside from our true center. He wished to set us an example; throughout His life, He had only one aim: to glorify His Father

---

[6] St. Ignatius of Loyola (1491-1556), founder of the Jesuit Order.

and thereby to teach us to seek within ourselves none save God alone. He made Himself as naught: all that counted was His Father's purpose.

And to make clearer the cost of this holy inner simplicity, and to help us to keep it, He chose a setting in life that proclaimed contempt for created things — those things which often lead us astray. A mode of life ruled by simplicity: simplicity of the manger; simplicity of the shepherds, His first adorers; simplicity of the life at Nazareth; simplicity of the Apostles; simplicity of life day by day. In that way, the interior and exterior would be in complete harmony; no misconception would be possible.

Our Lord would be simple to the extent that for thirty years He passed unnoticed, and when He entered upon His public life, the village folk would exclaim in amazement, "But this is the son of Joseph the carpenter! And it's He who talks like that and cures people! Would you believe it!"

The sanctity of Mary, too, was unobtrusive; no one among her neighbors in Nazareth had any idea of the treasures hidden within her. A young girl, quite unaffected; outwardly like everyone else; a young woman, modest and helpful, full of grace and passing unremarked. Her soul, though, was always perfectly simple, since her attitude toward God was never disturbed by the slightest attraction toward a creature. St. John of the Cross sums up the general doctrine when he declares, "From the beginning of her existence the glorious Mother of God found herself raised to a sublime state of union. Never in her soul was there the imprint of any created thing whatsoever, likely to distract her from God, or to move her in any act, seeing that she obeyed solely the guidance of the Holy Spirit."

Pope John Paul

---

[7] *Ascent of Mount Carmel*, Bk. 3, ch 1.

What simplicity there is also in St. Joseph, that artisan of a sanctity unrecorded, who ruled the divine Child without embarrassment and quite naturally, since that was the will of God.

The first disciples did not deceive themselves; they strove to practice inwardly this essential simplicity, to act only for God, and outwardly, like their Master, to practice simplicity in their daily conduct: "Whether you eat or drink, or whatsoever else you do, do all to the glory of God."[8] Such was their watchword one to another. It governed their inmost souls, and to confirm this inward attitude by a similar way of life, they lived as detached as possible from created things, even to sharing their goods in common. If later those outward exigencies of simplicity disappeared, at least the imperative rule remained: be poor in spirit — that is to say, detached from what is not God alone. Beatitude is promised to those who love nothing save God, desire only God, judge events only in relation to God — the triumph of that fundamental simplicity.

In modern times, certain souls, more numerous than one might believe, have given examples of true devotion to this essential simplicity. Mireille Dupouey, describing to a Benedictine priest how her husband lived before his complete return to the Christian life,[9] writes:

> I observed what it could mean in him, this effort to free himself, this reversal (if one may use the word) of all that he had been, an intellectual, a dilettante: a conversion to simplicity toward God, toward himself, toward everything. Without fully reckoning the mass of complexities that had brought it about, I saw that noble forehead bowed gently at

[8] 1 Cor. 10:31.

[9] Letter (dated May 14, 1923) quoted, together with the extracts that follow, in *La Vie Spirituelle* (January 1940): 50 ff.

the secret counsel of God, and heard him speak only of self-surrender, of confidence in God, of fidelity in His service and joy in His praise, whatever might befall.

She had believed when she became engaged that her companion for life had always been a practicing Catholic. This was incorrect; but what a joy it was to her to see him, after marriage, draw daily nearer the light; to hear him humbly asking her to explain a ritual of the Mass; to help him at his prayers, in his seeking for God by a resumed study of the Catechism and by familiarizing himself with the lovely lives of the saints.

She wrote from Brest to a friend:

No, Pierre had not explored all the secrets of the spiritual life. But after drifting aimlessly (rather like Gide) through years of unrestrained dilettantism with a ghastly sense of isolation, blankness, and emptiness, when he did receive the Faith he had no other thought than to give himself up to it like a child. He knew comparatively few things about the spiritual life, but these few things he took to heart and cherished. The things he learnt — or more truly, was given — came through simplicity and abandonment; and I believe that the radiance in him was (if I dare say it) a confirmation of the promise of our Lord: "If your eye is single, all your being will be in light."[10]

She adds, "I know nothing more attractive than the simplicity and self-surrender which he practiced and in which I now strive to live." One who later became the founder and director of *La Vie Spirituelle*, the Dominican Father Bernadot, wrote as a young man,

---

[10] Matt. 6:22.

"The great thing is to lend oneself to the divine purpose. No — I am wrong — to *give* oneself in complete trust and simplicity. At times God makes use of us in human, commonplace ways; at other times in work of an elevated order. The great thing is to remain His docile instruments." A few months before his death it is still simplicity that he stresses: "The spirit of Christ is found only in simple souls, in those who are without ambition." He believed that if he had to relive his life, he would — in view of the resources and limitations of his temperament, with its constant division between contemplation and activity — fall into the same difficulties as before; and he remarks that, being parted from the good works he had so much at heart, "it is better to end my life living in simplicity with Christ and His Mother."[11]

The biographer of Father Pernet, founder of the Little Sisters of the Assumption, and of Blessed Michael Garicoïts, founder of the Priests of the Sacred Heart at Betharram,[12] took pleasure in showing how the virtue of simplicity was characteristic of both their dispositions, claiming for them common sense, concord, and

[11] *Les 25 ans de la Vie Spirituelle*, 1919-1941 (Ed. du Cerf), 226, 232. Father Bernadot has given the best of his thought on spirituality in his well-known *De l'Eucharistie à la Trinité*.

[12] Gaétan Bernoville. See, e.g., *Vie du P. Pernet* (Grasset), 226. An incident on page 240 could serve as introduction to the pages that follow. Shortly after Father Pernet had founded the Little Sisters of the Assumption, one of the nuns read out to him the following maxim: "God is motionless. His existence cannot be disturbed; He lives in an infinite peace. It is for the sake of entering into that peace that we see so many souls, angelic rather than human, sever themselves from everything else to rest in Him." The Father was filled with admiration: "Ah, that is fine — a magnificent thought!" The nun told him the writer's name; it was himself. "What! Did *I* say that? Surely not! Quite impossible!" And neither his forgetfulness nor his surprise affected his serenity.

Holy Simplicity

prudence; the ability to live as one thinks and to think conformably to the pure logic of a love that can ensure unity; to reject instinctively all complexity, affectation, and display — a remote image, but one already very clear, of the essential attribute which is the perfection even of God.

Chapter 2

∞

The Simple Soul Is
Natural in All Its Ways

In studying simplicity, one may begin with God; here we are on the metaphysical plane. One may begin with a child — when the approach is, let us say, rather more psychological. After the supreme greatness of God Himself, to study what is least of all, a child, seems an odd way of learning; but then, has not our Lord Himself bidden us to do it? "*Nisi efficiamini:* Unless you become as little children, ye shall not enter into the kingdom of Heaven."[13]

A child is so clearly what he is, without subterfuge, complexity, or restraint of any kind. He fears nothing and no one. He is ready to be friendly with all; what he offers, he gives freely. He is all impulse, spontaneity; no reflection embarrasses or checks him, or prompts him how to behave — he is frankly what he is. If he can talk, he instinctively speaks the truth unless his elders have taught him to fib; he is straightforward, and cannot believe that anyone would deceive him; everything is a source of wonder to him; he is swift in admiration. If he asks questions, it is not to argue but to learn; and he believes what he is told. He knows that he is weak,

[13] Matt. 18:3.

and he is not lessened thereby; he pins his faith on those around him, and in his weakness lies his strongest sway.

Let us first give the negative definition of simplicity in this aspect: later we shall come to the positive.

∞

Fénelon writes as follows: "Simplicity is a rectitude of the soul which takes away all futile looking into itself or its actions" — "*oculus simplex*" as the *Imitation* expresses it; whereby, once the vision is fixed on an object, there is no attempt at the same time to consider anything to right or left, and still less any tendency to introspection.

St. Louis[14] counseled his children: "Fair sons, be loyal, veering neither to the right hand nor to the left, but ever straight on."

In humility, unless it has reached its fullest scope, as in our Lady, there is still a turning back upon oneself, either to disclose defects or to reproach oneself for them.[15] He who is simple forgets about himself, and without having to make an effort at self-forgetfulness. He does not think about himself; his attention is fixed solely on the action or purpose at issue. Because of this, the virtue of simplicity has an attractiveness that is lacking in humility. Humility is cautious; she watches her step; she never lets herself go or relaxes self-scrutiny. Simplicity pursues her own course; she is not preoccupied; she knows no alarm or uneasiness, much less self-conceit. If she should attract notice or happen to be praised, she accepts attention and praise with good grace. What is the use of crossing swords

---

[14] St. Louis IX (1214-1270), king of France.

[15] See in the *Revue d'Ascétique et de Mystique*, July 1924, in which Father Joseph de Guibert explains how the saints could believe in all truth that they were the last among men (*Humilité et Vérité*, 217-233).

or hiding in one's tent? Never mind — no harm is done — see for yourself how it glances off without penetrating. So why be troubled by it? When Cardinal Mercier met Marshal Foch in Brussels at the end of the War of 1914-1918 and congratulated him, Foch replied, "We are all merely the instruments of Providence."

It is said that Katherine Mansfield, that sensitive novelist, once admitted to her husband: "When people praise me, I always long to fall on my knees and beg God to make me better." There is a fine "simplicity." But is there not a simplicity even more simple — that of one who pays no heed whatsoever to praise?

Two pleasing touches in the life of the Bishop of Geneva:[16] Once, when in Avignon, he was recognized in the street and compliments were showered upon him. He took refuge in a bookseller's shop on the pretext of examining the volumes, and said wistfully, "How gladly I would do something ridiculous to disillusion these good people! Yet one must not play the sage or the fool, but live in Christian sincerity."

Another time, at the Visitation at Lyons, he was talking to the Superior, Mother de Blonay. St. Francis de Sales was not well. The nuns noticed that the door of the parlor stood ajar; Monseigneur might catch a chill. The prelate took heed of the warning, and stood up — then promptly sat down again: "Out there is a crowd of little children looking at me so trustfully that I have not the heart to shut the door in their faces."[17]

Many fail in simplicity through a certain tendency to self-esteem. They nurse their reputation. When taking action, they ask themselves in what light they will appear most favorably, and reap the greatest measure of approbation. Here the duality is flagrant, as it

[16] St. Francis de Sales (1567-1622).
[17] Trochu, *Life of Saint Francis de Sales*, II, 697, 703.

is in those human considerations that stifle action between the dictates of conscience and fear of public opinion.

Others lack simplicity because they habitually pass everything through a sieve of criticism that suppresses all spontaneity. The instant an impulse is born, a paralyzing reflex springs up — "Is that all right? Would it be better to do something else?" — and this can become, as in some scrupulous types, a constant fluctuation. Here the attention is not entirely on the action to be taken or the movement to be made; it rests equally on what one should perhaps do and is not doing. Again and always a division, a dualism. Simplicity is not in this.

Many lack simplicity through sheer timidity. In an irrational fear of themselves or others, they advance, draw back, hesitate, become motionless again — and then a second later go through the whole performance once more. One longs to say to them, "Get on with it! Do what you are going to do; don't be continually moving about like a concertina, not knowing which note to settle on!"

Some forms of timidity are congenital or come from an upbringing that has been too repressive, devitalizing instead of invigorating; but there are also types of timidity that spring from a lurking pride, the fear of appearing ridiculous. Happy are they who know how to free themselves from such bogeys.

∞

The virtue of simplicity excludes all useless turning back upon oneself, which would in fact be duality; but that is only the negative aspect.

More positively, simplicity consists in a certain transparency of soul; perfect naturalness in all circumstances and before everyone; a gift of freshness, detached and entirely open; of frankness that is not merely artlessness, but trust in God and our neighbors; a faculty of wonder and an innate tendency toward admiration, because everything appears great to the great, pure to the pure.

To secure the fullest perception of perfect simplicity in this sense, nothing could be better than to consider one or another of the great exponents of this virtue. Certainly all the saints have, in their own way, practiced simplicity, at least of the type discussed in the preceding chapter. But no one will dispute that the most outstanding examples of the childlike simplicity with which we are now concerned have been provided by such as Thérèse of the Child Jesus, Bernadette, Francis of Assisi, John Baptist Vianney, and many others like them.[18]

Of "Little Thérèse" a lay-sister asked, "What can they write about her after her death?" That good woman looked only at the surface and could not gauge the depths.[19]

And what can be said of the humble troubador of God, the Seraph of Assisi, he who gave orders with the utmost naturalness to the wolf, the birds, the frogs; the poet of the "Canticle of the Sun"; the lover of stark poverty; the friend of beggars and lepers; the recluse who loved the forests of Alvernia and the caves of Monte Subasio; the herald of Christ the King, whose sole dream it was to live and make his brethren live *secundum formam sancti Evangelii* — according to the rule outlined in the gospel?

---

[18] St. Thérèse of Lisieux (1873-1897), French Carmelite nun and Doctor; St. Bernadette Soubirous (1844-1879), Sister of Notre Dame who, in 1858, received eighteen apparitions of the Blessed Virgin Mary at Lourdes in France; St. Francis of Assisi (1182-1226), founder of the Franciscan Order; St. John Vianney (1786-1859), patron saint of parish priests, known as the Curé d'Ars.

[19] "Little Thérèse" was certainly true to type in her vocation; the "Great St. Teresa" (St. Teresa of Avila) used to say, "The day you cease to be simple, I shall disown you as my daughters."

Holy Simplicity

The word *simple,* as Joergensen says, in a meditation dated from the Portiuncula, 1926,[20] is among those which occur most frequently from the pen and on the lips of the Poor Man of Assisi. "Simply and with few words" he had written that first rule of life which he was to present to the great Innocent III in Rome. And the Pope, from whom he begged approbation of the Portiuncula Indulgence, called him *"simplicissimus"* — greatly simple — so markedly was the first impression that the character of St. Francis made one of inexpressible candor.

If the Poverello in the thirteenth century could win so many hearts beguiled by false values, swamped by futile needs and vain cravings for wealth and luxury, if he could turn them from the path to damnation, which one of his biographers rightly calls "the endless path of desires" (*viam interminabilem desideriorumit*), it is certainly due to the virtue of simplicity carried to the extent of heroism.

In the life of the illustrious martyr St. Thomas More (1478-1535), Lord Chancellor of England, we see him at the peak of his career, serving Mass like a young acolyte, clad in a surplice, chanting in choir with the priests, and carrying the cross before others in processions.

No more need be said about the simplicity of St. Francis de Sales. The example of simplicity in other saints charmed him. On October 14, 1604, he wrote to Madame de Chantal: "Father Ignatius Loyola, who will be canonized, ate meat on Ash Wednesday when so ordered by his doctor, who thought it necessary for a

---

[20] Republished in the *Messager du Coeur de Jésus* (October 1926). Many could be cited as following Francis of Assisi. Brother Leo, for instance, or Giles or Pacificus, of whom the *Fioretti* tell us. The latter were not great scholars; yet such a man as St. Bonaventure would seek from them explanation of points of theology — so greatly is God's grace given to simple souls.

slight ailment of his. A more constrained spirit would have had to be coaxed for three days!"

Less well known is the good old doorkeeper of the College in Majorca, St. Alphonsus Rodriguez, who had been a merchant and was not uncultured, but whose simplicity seemed one of his most delightful characteristics. One day our Lady told him that she loved him. "Oh," he retorted, "not as much as I love you!" On another occasion, when at recreation, he thought he heard his superior order him to go to India. At once he prepared to set off, and when the position was explained to him, and he was asked what he would have done if he could not find a ship ready to sail: "I should have gone into the water and not come ashore until I had proved that I could go no further."[21]

A fine example of simplicity is that of a lad of eighteen whom Father Surin met in a coach from Rouen (letter of May 8, 1630). This lad spoke to him openly and freely of the amazing wonders God had worked within him. "Through his simplicity," wrote Surin to his instructor of the third year, Brother Louis Lallemant, "I discovered in him great marvels, and his simplicity hid from me many more besides." The complete document is still extant.[22]

Simplicity is not a matter of rank; if vulgarity signifies vain pretension, one can be vulgar in any rank of society. Certainly it is not impossible, as we remarked at the outset, to find pleasant examples of simplicity in persons of the highest rank and the noblest extraction. Wherever there is breeding, as we call it, one finds that

---

[21] On another occasion, the conversation turned to swimming. He was asked, "Do *you* know how to swim?" "Why, yes." And lying on a bench (others say on the ground), he proceeded to demonstrate with rhythmical movements of arms and legs.

[22] The first in any edition of the *Letters of Père Surin*. It is so well known that it has often been published separately.

easy dignity which, far from keeping aloof, puts one at ease, attracts, and prevails. But it may be that we more easily discern a more exquisite simplicity in a setting that hints at and exacts a total absence of vanity and ambition.

Take the not uncommon case of a countrywoman, who, to rear her many children and fill the place of a sick husband, goes to bed at eleven, gets up at three, and answers a suggestion that she is overworking with, "Did not God tell us to work by the sweat of our brows?" She lets her eldest son enter the Seminary at a time when he could have assisted her; loses her second son; preserves her confidence despite it all; controls her household with rare skill, never for a moment thinks much of it, saying, "It's very simple; there's nothing else to be done." She deserves this fine tribute from one observer: "What struck me most in her was her great goodness, her courage; but even more an absence of virtue which long seemed mysterious to me: that way of thinking her conduct quite natural, that easy, spontaneous — fundamental, one could call it — way of welcoming her life and living it. Really, one never saw her behave otherwise!"

"Absence of virtue": it would be better to say *absence of display in the practice of virtue*. In fact, exceptional virtue, with the rare merit of being unaware of itself.

One cannot fail to recall, from a different category but still in the direct line of the noblest simplicity, this reply by the painter Corot, then eighty years old, on being asked the secret of the lasting freshness of his landscapes: "Every day I ask God to make me a child — that is, that He may make me see nature and depict it as a child would."

Or again, this exquisite phrase from the Breton sailor Jean-Marie Cadiou, sole survivor of the *Amiral-Carner*, which went down two minutes after being torpedoed off the Syrian coast on

February 8, 1916. For five days, Cadiou drifted on a raft. His thirteen companions died; but he, with his eyes fixed on the East and the land where the Cross once stood, did not despair. After five days, he was picked up and, when recovered, was sent for by the admiral. Asked, "What did you think about during those long hours?" he replied, "I prayed all the time."

The biographers of Bernadette have recorded how the girl, at the time of the apparitions, passed with charming unaffectedness through the crowds gathered at Massabieille before her arrival; how, with those who reproached her, gendarmes or commissioners, as well as with those who praised her, she kept a serene expression and showed neither alarm nor complacency. She was still the good little country lass they had all known until then. One can glean in her life numerous occasions where her shrewdness in some respects was linked with simplicity. An old priest asked her one day, "Is it true that you have seen the Blessed Virgin?" "Yes, Monsieur l'Abbé." "Well, I don't believe you have seen her." "Oh, she did not tell me to make people believe it."

On her Profession Day, with the Sisters of Nevers, a little scene had been staged. All her companions were allotted their functions; she had none. Msgr. Forcade asked her, "So, you are no use at all?" "Mother General is quite right; it's quite true." "Then what good was it for you to enter this congregation?" "That's just what I said to you at Lourdes, and you told me it didn't matter."

At the end of her life, she was obliged to follow a diet; the cook had no patience with it. "Did her mother give her chicken every day?" "No, but what my mother gave me she gave with all her heart."[23]

---

[23] Petitot, *Histoire exacte de in vie extérieure et religieuse de sainte Bernadette* (Desclée de Brouwer), 58, 130, 179.

Chapter 3

∞

The Soul's Relationship with God

Let us consider the simple soul in its relations with God, with its neighbor, and with itself.

First of all, with God.

The simple soul has understood the *unum necessarium*: unity is what is needed — God alone. It may and will have numerous occupations; but in everything, it seeks and sees nothing but its Lord. As our Lord, in the midst of His numerous occupations, His journeyings, His preaching, the cures He wrought, His varied apostolate, His sufferings, had one sole aim: to glorify His beloved Father — "Behold, I come to do Thy will";[24] "my meat is to do the will of Him that sent me"[25] — so will the soul that lives in simplicity be unconcerned by changes in its tasks. It is not a question of wishing (unduly) to please its neighbor or to satisfy itself, but of the will of God. "Amen. *Ita Pater*. Not my will, but Thine."

Good directors strive to lead the souls in their charge to this state, and when the Duchess of York repeats to Mother Croiset,

---

[24] Heb. 10:9.
[25] John 4:34.

23

Holy Simplicity

Superior of the Visitation of Chaillot, the counsels given her by her chaplain, Father de la Colombière, she writes:

> Among other counsels he bade me ponder much the need I had of simplifying myself inwardly so as to care for nothing save God, in spite of the multiplicity of things surrounding me; that God desired from me this readiness to give Him back my entire self and all that concerned me to do with as He would; that I should pay less heed to what I had done than to what I ought to do; which would make me pliant and docile to the commands of the providence of God in such events as He might ordain.[26]

There is one aim only: to please God. Anything else will be a diversion, in the Pascalian sense of the word. There must be one motive-force only: love. The simple soul is not of those who live in fear, as if they served a harsh and ruthless master: it says with Marie-Antoinette de Geuser, "Purgatory and Hell do not trouble me in the least" — not because it ignores their existence or believes itself confirmed in grace, but because it possesses a hope steadfast enough to refrain from even a momentary doubt of love — simplicity.

It is not disturbed by its own infidelities — faults of slight gravity — since we assume this is a fervent soul. It does its best to reduce them; but, if it has a failure, it repents immediately, without checking its progress or imitating those hopeless people who, at the first tumble — often enough almost involuntary — pause by the way, feel themselves all over, take stock of themselves, and are childishly surprised at their weakness, as if

[26] Quoted in Georges Guitton's life of Claude de la Colombière (Vine), 387.

their good intentions, obvious enough, should have made them infallible.

The simple soul is not disconcerted; it has due regard for its unbecoming conduct, but is not over-troubled unless willfulness has a part in it. It makes use of the experience to gain a surer foothold in humility, losing nothing of its happiness and comforting itself with the thought that God will be all the more God in its own case since it has given Him — unintentionally, of course — the chance to show greater mercy.[27]

A soul of holiness does not strive for that holiness. It strives to love, to love wholeheartedly; there lies the difference. In the desire for sanctity there is still a deviation of motive. The simple soul loves; that is all. It would love still more. "My cup is full, but I could wish it were greater," as Marie-Antoinette de Geuser put it. Even that wish leaves it serene and untroubled. It knows itself in all its nakedness, and if it finds in itself something that is good, it esteems this gift of God as wonderful without any personal vanity. It knows that of itself it can do nothing; but that knowledge does not distress it, anymore than a child is distressed by his helplessness. When he slips, he keeps no count of it. Does a mother count

[27] The widow of Pierre Dupouey, to whom we referred earlier, explains this very well in a letter to a friend who lived in a state of chronic anxiety: "We must be very simple with God . . . must not be ever telling Him of our troubles . . . Just as we must weep for displeasing God, so we must bear ourselves in simplicity and almost joyfully. Our misfortunes may — if we are simple and upright — become one of the foundations of our humility and adoration, instead of being always a source of complaint and discouragement. The danger is not so much in being unhappy, as in analyzing one's unhappiness . . . In the second book of the *Imitation* there is an exquisite chapter on 'simplicity and purity of heart,' which I never read without benefit, and which might perhaps help you, too" (letter of May 14, 1923, quoted in *La Vie Spirituelle* [January 1940]: 57-58).

how many times her child tumbles in learning to walk? And is not God better than the best of mothers?

A fine instance of this simplicity toward God is to be found in the Abbé Rémy Pasteau, killed in action on Pentecost, 1940. He wrote from the Front, thinking of the account that might soon have to be rendered: "It is so simple not to worry anymore about the past, even about the faults and negligences for which one pays now by no longer hiding all one owes, or about that future, which nothing allows us to foresee or to plan. It is so simple now to have nothing now in view but the presence of God and our presence before Him."

He does not use that last phrase casually; his love makes everything simple. He goes on: "We must remember one thing only; it is indeed the only final reality: the immense, marvelous, and almost impossible love that God in His goodness has toward us. Why, then, should one linger over so many paltry trifles?"

He thrusts aside all anxiety — better still, he defies it — for his inward attitude keeps it from even grazing him. "Is not this true happiness: to know that one can count on nothing today, tomorrow, that last day of all, save only this tenderness, this love — this one supreme love?"[28]

Another example of simplicity toward God is that of Guy de Larigaudie, as revealed in the notes published after his death.[29] He wished to "make his life a conversation with God." He has in mind that he is a sportsman and a lover of the open air when he outlines this most simple and familiar contact with the Father who is in Heaven:

[28] *Construire, XIV, Vigile sons les acmes* — Daniélou, 122, 126, 130, 134.

[29] Published as *Etoiles au grand large,* with introduction by Father Forestier, O.P., by Editions du Seuil, Paris.

As one flicks the top off wild carrot with a riding-crop, chews a grass-stem, or shaves in the morning, one can keep on telling God without tiring of it, quite simply, that one loves Him well — and that is worth just as much as all the floods of tears ever poured out in pious tomes. Hum over all that the past has given, all that dreams shape for the days ahead, and in that song speak to God. Speak to Him again as you dance with joy in the sunlight; on the beach; or as you speed over the snow on skis. Have God always close, as a companion to whom one can entrust oneself.

Once he narrowly escaped being drowned; he writes:

In a flash I was aware of all my life. But I had no time for regret or any kind of contrition. I said inwardly with a force that stifled every other feeling, "I am not worth much, Lord; but all the same I have loved You well." That was all. There was no trace of alarm in me. Only an immense joy.

What perfectly simple serenity at the thought of soon appearing before God! He does not speak in fear, but with the trust of a son.

I came to realize that there is really only one thing in the world that matters — the love of God, an immense, unreasoning love, like the adoration of a lad for his mother; a love which claims us wholly at every moment of our lives; which wipes out all our blemishes and remains sole and triumphant. Since that day I no longer dread a sudden death — though, of course, I would rather die in full awareness. I would rather take my whole life into the hollow of my hands, and offer it to Him as my humble, human gift. But it would be just as good if, instead of opening slowly upon the light, the door were flung wide suddenly.

Holy Simplicity

Let us admire the sound spiritual health behind those spontaneous phrases in which the writer showed himself as he was. How many troubled or complex souls would do well to take him as an example![30]

Actually, not everyone possesses this inborn faculty for free expression. St. Francis Borgia[31] was full of holiness. Yet, despite the ease with which he disentangled the temporal affairs of his duchy of Gandia while he was still in the world, and later the spiritual concerns of the Society of Jesus as its Superior General, he had to fight down a certain tendency toward introversion. His best biographer, Father Suau, mentions that in his own spiritual life he was rather prone to worry, and that, to be freed from this, he frequently prayed to God that he might be enabled to walk *in simplicitate cordis* — in simplicity of heart.

The Abbé Long-Hasselmans, of whom we shall speak later, a highly distinguished priest of Marseilles who unfortunately died young, blamed himself, as a student of theology at the Gregorian University in Rome, for an injurious tendency to introspection:

> I am completely worn out by so many complications. I used to think them a sign of profoundness; but the living spirit is not to be found there. God is infinitely simple. My complexity — all complexity — is born of a mixture: I want to combine God — the highest asceticism — with the world, the most subtle pleasures. Naturally that is no simple undertaking.
>
> . . . Simple as the dove: I belong to God.

---

[30] This calm recalls that of Father Faber, who asked for Holy Communion on the day he died; on being refused it, because he was too weak, he asked for *The Pickwick Papers*.

[31] St. Francis Borgia (1510-1572), Duke of Gandia who became a Jesuit, established the order throughout western Europe, and sent missionaries to the Americas.

I live for God. No subtlety. This is pleasing to God — I will do it; this is not pleasing to God — I will not do it.

And I am perfectly certain that I shall lose nothing: a simple soul strikes a clearer, more compelling note. A complex soul pleases itself only, and that not for long: it interests others, again not for long — and then it wearies everybody.

The task is not so much to learn as to unlearn: one must put aside conventions and ready-made phrases; see our Lord as He is and lay ourselves at His feet as we really are.[32]

In this way, one could trace the portrait of the soul that is simple toward God: virtuous, without imagining it; prayerful, without splitting hairs over the exact form or quality of its prayer; loving without consideration of anything but the object of its love; going ahead without troubling to mark the stages or ascertain its own progress. If a confessor, or the Holy Spirit, has given instructions or suggested the writing down of some inspiration, the simple soul will carry it out; but it will do so calmly, as if it were speaking of someone else — never, of course, to scrutinize itself or to pride itself on the grace it has received. "If thy eye be single, thy whole body shall be lightsome," our Lord said.[33] In the simple soul the gaze is wholly clear; any oblique glance is excluded.

∞

In prayer, the simple soul can dispense with many considerations; its intellect fixes on the sole light, and the chance reflections, which are excellent for others, are a hindrance rather than a help. Spiritual writers have defined this mode of prayer as "the

---

[32] Ludovic Giraud, *Vie* (Marseilles: Publiroc), 51-52.
[33] Matt. 6:22.

prayer of simplicity." It consists in a loving attention toward God, varying in intensity, in freedom from distraction, and in length, springing forth more or less spontaneously and not needing to nourish itself by any separate or especially varied acts.

This does not imply that all souls that strive to practice the virtue of simplicity, or that practice it spontaneously, necessarily comply with this form of prayer, but that they tend toward it unconsciously, at least in its lower forms.[34] And if the Holy Spirit sometimes seems to direct them toward a more elaborate form of prayer, one which calls for different thoughts, the simple soul is not dismayed and does not ask for explanation. God, who guides all things, is the Master; He will restore it, when He wills, to the sweetness of a more peaceful intimacy.

The more a soul simplifies itself, the more God works in it; and, conversely, the more God works in it, the simpler does the soul become. The spiritual writers St. John of the Cross and St. Teresa[35] have carefully studied this plasticity of the soul under divine action when the successive purgations have prepared the ground, and we cannot do better than refer to their descriptions. In the outcome the divine Master has taken possession of the soul. The "ego" appears definitely nonexistent. It is the fullness of liberty, the self with its tangles and brambles no longer attempting (or at least not succeeding, for it can still make itself felt in the imagination or the emotions) to disturb the resolute unity.

---

[34] For there is a whole range. In the *Revue d'Ascétique et de Mystique*, Father de Grandmaison devotes a whole article to "*La forme faible de l'oraison de simplicité*"(I, 49).

[35] St. John of the Cross (1542-1591) and St. Teresa of Avila (1515-1582), Spanish Carmelite mystics who reformed the Carmelite Order.

"Between God and the soul," the Master once explained, "all that is not God is a constraint, a hindrance to union." And again, "Take everything which leads thee to me, and leave all the rest."[36] It is a complete dispossession and cannot be attained without having done violence to the self. How generous one must be to exact from oneself a lively and active cooperation in the despoiling workings of God; to let oneself be torn away from — or to tear away from oneself — every kind of multiplicity.

When, at the consecration of the Mass, the words of the priest replace the elements of bread with the substance of Christ, all happens in a moment; the bread is inert matter; no fragment of it resists. But when it is a question of a soul becoming — if one dare say it — transubstantiated into Jesus Christ, it is understandable that there is cause for struggle. If "I" is to die, there must be many deaths: victory is only for the valiant.

We have stressed the conduct of the simple soul at prayer, as was natural. Its piety in other forms is marked by special characteristics. It no longer needs a wide range of pious practices; does not seek to increase or to vary its prayers, preferring rather to live its life as one single prayer.

In his *Mysticism of the Earth*, Father Pascal quotes the method of prayer of the Venerable Marie- Celeste Crostarosa, who assisted St. Alphonsus Liguori in founding his order.[37] Our Lord had told her as a child. "Look at the sun, how it gives light, warms the plants into growth so that they bear flowers and fruit, and how it

---

[36] Poulain, *Le journal de Lucie-Christine*, 2nd ed. (Beauchesne, 1912), 159.

[37] St. Alphonsus Liguori (1696-1787), bishop, Doctor, writer, and founder of the Redemptorists.

gladdens the whole world . . . It is the symbol of my divine presence." She followed the flight of birds; pondered over the flowers and other things in nature — an excellent way to rise toward God and one that St. Ignatius of Loyola recommends in his Rules and his "Exercise on the Love of God" at the end of the *Spiritual Exercises*.

In the use of devotions, the simple soul seeks for nothing unusual or original. It goes straight for what is essential, and, on occasion, shares in popular devotions rather than appear aloof. Shortly after Jean-François de Sales had been named coadjutor to his elder brother, Monseigneur de Genève was invited for St. Anthony's feast by the Franciscans. He set out immediately and, on his return, was rallied by his brother: "As I see it, you are like those simple women who rush to burn a candle to St. Anthony when they mislay a distaff." The elder gently put his younger brother in his place, and then, as if regretting the reproof, he added smilingly, "Suppose we both made a vow to St. Anthony for the recovery of what we lose daily — you, Christian simplicity; and I, humility?"[38]

When it is not a matter of example or charity and the soul can follow its own bent, there is no cause for surprise if in its intimate life it refrains from one or another voluntary devotion. It seems to shock some to learn that St. Catherine of Genoa,[39] so zealous in praying for the souls in Purgatory, could not, at one stage of her life, take thought over gaining indulgences. She in no way condemned this devotion, excellent in itself; it was simply that she had no inclination toward it.

[38] Trochu, *Life of Saint Francis de Sales*, ch. 2, 668.

[39] St. Catherine of Genoa (1447-1510), mystic and writer who ministered to the sick at a Genoese hospital.

The saints in general are moderate in their devotions; they value all that are approved by the Church, but do not feel obliged to make use of all. A biographer of St. Teresa of Avila, Henry Joly,[40] recalls this saying of the great reformer of Carmel: "I am not one to bless myself." We can guess in what sense she meant those words to be taken.

Pauline Martin had given her sister, "Little Thérèse," a notebook for marking the sacrifices made in preparation for her First Communion; they reached a total of 818. Later Sister Thérèse of the Child Jesus was to say that these multiplications of acts were no longer necessary to her. Perfection does not really consist in multiplying practices, however excellent they may be. We must not condemn those who have that type of devotion and choose to take on more than we do, like Father Doyle[41] or some of the Desert Fathers — Paul the monk, for example, who said 300 prayers a day, marking each with a small pebble, and was very mortified to learn that a village girl had achieved 700.

Besides, Father Doyle did not encourage in others that multiplication of practices and overwhelming penances. The early ascetics, too, favored a wise restraint. "The monk who lives in simplicity and innocence," wrote Cassian, "will be sustained by the most sublime mysteries, not through piling up his repetitions of the Psalms, but through being inspired by the sentiments expressed in the Psalms."

"There is no need of many words," St. Macarius explained. "It is enough to lift one's hands toward Heaven and to say, 'Thy will be done, O Lord.' "

---

[40] Collection, *Les Saints* (Gabalda), 23.

[41] There is an interesting article by Father de Grandmaison on this unusual Irish army chaplain in the *Revue d'Ascétique et de Mystique* (April 1921): 128-146.

Pambon in his youth was given as counsel a text from the Bible; he meditated on it for nineteen years without taking any other subject.[42]

In short the principle remains: stability and moderation are worth more than triviality and superfluity.

---

[42] Jean Bremond, *Les Pères du Desert*, in the collection *Les Moralistes chrétiens* (Gabalda), Vol. II, 469, 485, 528, 530.

Chapter 4

The Soul's Relationship with Its Neighbor

The simple soul remains in the sight of all men as it is before God. It behaves before others no differently than if God alone beheld it; therefore it does not pretend or seek to hide anything or to draw attention to one course it may follow rather than to another. And if it sees it is esteemed more than is reasonable, so far from an inner sensation of pleasure, it will feel distress at it. If it feels it is loved, it realizes that this may be on account of its good qualities — and certainly in spite of its defects; and rejoices at it, thanking God, without developing any conceit for itself. If it is a great source of edification, it is precisely because it has never sought for the edification of others by pretending to be other than it is. It is the pure radiance in which the simple soul moves freely that warms and illuminates.

This inward simplicity will show itself in many ways.

Simplicity in dress — that is the exterior. It matters less than the interior, but nevertheless, it matters. Simplicity adapts itself to its position. St. Louis considered his queen too well attired; the queen wished that the king would dress more fittingly. When St.

Holy Simplicity

Francis de Sales was first shown the habit designed for the Visitation nuns, he took the scissors and shortened the veil at the ends. While still at home, St. Jane Frances de Chantal was dismayed by her daughters' taste for finery; the bishop told her, "It is right for pheasants to preen themselves." But if one of the girls was over-stylish, his rebuke could strike a chill through the fine feathers. He wished his "devout woman" to be well-dressed, not from ostentation, but so that virtue might be associated with good taste.

∞

Simplicity in conversation: Our Lord bids us, "When you speak, say what is, is; what is not, is not." Nothing should be studied or affected. "When you are before the judges, you will say what the Holy Spirit inspires you to say."

St. Vincent de Paul told his daughters: "You will know if you are truly Sisters of Charity if you are all simple; not set in your opinions, but submissive to those of others; frank in your speech, without your hearts thinking one thing while your lips frame another."

To the Priests of the Mission he repeated the same counsel: "In our speech, the tongue must express things outwardly just as we hold them inwardly; otherwise we must keep silence." To his two religious families, he offered his own example: "For myself, God has given me so great an esteem for simplicity that I call it my gospel. I find a special devotion and consolation in speaking of things as they are."[43]

Always courteous, and with nothing casual in it, simplicity is in no way synonymous with negligence or undue familiarity. Yet it

---

[43] Louis Déplanque, *Saint Vincent de Paul sous l'emprise chrétienne,* 226, 267. *Œuvres complètes de S. V. de P.* (Ed. Coste), IX, 81, 606.

loathes the deceitful artificiality of worldly manners, which it does not mistake for true politeness. Simplicity has little use for endless protests as to who shall have precedence in passing through a door;[44] it has respect for those lower in rank, because it looks behind appearances and sees God. With people of position, it is unmoved and unconcerned, believing God alone is great. On every occasion, the simple soul spontaneously finds the right gesture, and nearly always with a touch of naturalness that gives an added charm. What delightful little scenes could be sketched from the lives of the early monks and the old solitaries!

Someone once asked Abbot Poemen, "What should one do if a brother falls asleep during Office?" "I myself," said he, "if I see a brother sleeping, take his head on my lap and help him to have his rest."

A solitary calls to see another. "Forgive me," he says as he takes his leave, "for having made you break silence." "My rule," answers the other, "is to practice the virtue of hospitality, and to receive with all kindness those who come to see me."

An old anchorite who was ill had a fancy for some fresh bread. One of his brethren set off at once, hurried across the desert, and returned as fast as he could. Out of regard for austerity, the old man refused the bread. "Take it, in the Lord's name. You must not let your brother's sacrifice go for naught." And in all simplicity, the sick man accepted the loaf.[45]

---

[44] One may recall the story of the two saintly men who each wished to kneel to the other when they met. The more active one succeeded, and the other remarked simply, "You are the more humble, and I the more humbled."

[45] See J. Bremond, *Les Pères du Désert*, in the collection *Les Moralistes chrétiens* (Gabalda), II, 306, 354, 359. Sometimes the desire for mortification overcame simplicity, as on the occasion when a worthy infirmarian made a mistake in his jars, and used rancid lamp oil instead of honey on an old man's bread. It was only at the

Holy Simplicity

Of course, the simple soul never includes in its talk anything that might go to make it esteemed beyond its worth, to build it into a legend or to win "a place in history"; nothing to cloak in unconscious artfulness its incapacity, its blunders, or negligence, hiding imperfections and keeping some aspect of personality discreetly shadowed. How few know us as we really are! How instinctively we barricade ourselves in; how jealously we defend our inner fortress! How few know what we really think! When we are faced with a view opposed to our own, how skilled we are, through politeness or diplomacy, in not revealing our real position. So that our opponent possibly finishes by believing us to be more or less in agreement with him, because we know so well how to tone down our contrasting view and take the edge off all our opposition.

We take an interest in somebody; we are generous of words; but how much real sincerity is there behind them? What is left once you scrape away the formal and conventional?

It would, indeed, never occur to the simple soul to disparage itself with any direct or indirect idea of appearing virtuous: it instinctively practices the advice of Fénelon: "Humble silence is better than humble speech." If there are religious people who (unhappily, says Faber) seek to achieve humility by striving to be misjudged, there is no danger that the simple soul will take them as examples. That type of virtue does not appeal to it.[46] It is aware of its real defects and is not concerned with manufacturing more.

third meal, when he saw the old man retching and tasted the horrible stuff himself, in an attempt to give encouragement, that the poor fellow became aware of his mistake.

[46] Nor apparently to our Lord, to judge by the revelation recounted by Father de Foucauld (*Ecrits Spirituels*, 110): "So much the better if men look on you as mad . . . but do nothing to provoke this — nothing strange or eccentric . . . I have done nothing to be treated so."

The Soul's Relationship with Its Neighbor

In the life of Don Bosco we find the story of how he was on one occasion invited out for a meal, at which some people expected him to do no more than toy with his food. On the contrary, when he came to the sweet, he took a normal helping — possibly even above the normal. Whereon one lady whispered to her neighbor, "You can see he is a saint, for he wants us to think he is not. What humility!" Nothing so complicated had ever occurred to Don Bosco. In fact, when he was told of it later, he commented with a smile, "The really important thing is to enjoy a good reputation. If you have that, you can do anything."[47]

When kindliness or even the interest of conversation demands it, the simple soul will not refuse to say honestly what it knows. It will take part willingly, in the knowledge that, while the "self" is to be detested, the obstinate refusal to show nothing of that self can become a form of pride, or at least a bar to kindness. While some people have an intolerable tendency to burden all conversation with their own interests, others have a habit, which detracts from the interest of their talk, of speaking of things as if they were no concern of theirs. Simplicity is prepared to talk about

[47] Quoted in Auffray's *Un saint traverse la France* (Vitte), 188. Together with zeal, simplicity was a virtue very dear to Don Bosco. One day he visited the Superior of the Little Sisters of the Assumption, who was ill. She asked him to bless her house, and to pray God to allow her to live longer, so that she might strengthen the bases of her foundation. "Why, yes," replied Don Bosco. "I will ask that you may live as long as Methuselah — 969 years." On the poor Superior's exclaiming at this, he suggested, "All right, we will drop the first figure! In return, pray that Don Bosco may save his soul." "And that you may live as long as I." "Oh, if I lived as long as Methuselah, I should turn the world upside down. And, if you lived 969 years, what progress there would be in your order! When you and I are both in Heaven, I shall ask God for a place a little apart — for I and all my noisy vagabonds would trouble your peace."

itself if necessary (and no more than necessary) if it sees that its neighbor is interested; but it never has any wish to win esteem in so doing.[48]

As for concealing thought, the simple soul does not feel bound to tell all its thoughts to everyone, for true simplicity is discreet and does not run counter to the innate good sense that tells it what is better said and what left unsaid; anyone talking with such a person will feel that he is trusted and believed, and will not have any feeling that the listener is attempting to get at his hidden thoughts, his character, or his limitations. There will be no trace of assumed politeness, false in itself and based on hypocrisy. When the simple soul says that it loves, it is because it does love; if it says it has trust, it is because that trust is there. There is in it nothing of the duality that we call "duplicity."[49]

If we believe Estelle Faguette, the visionary of Pellevoisin in Indre, the subject of a miraculous cure in 1876, the Holy Virgin at

---

[48] Recall, for instance, Saint Paul's "I have labored more abundantly than all they, yet not I but the grace of God with me. But by the grace of God I am what I am" (1 Cor. 15:10). Again, elsewhere, he has no hesitation in calling himself a small man; in fact, to give the Greek word its full force, the smallest of the small (Eph. 3:8; 1 Cor. 15:9).

[49] We have already alluded to the simplicity of Mary. Let me finish with these few lines of S. Joffroy in *Cahiers de Sainte Jehanne* (May 1935): "The Holy Virgin was always true in her conversations and her friendships; she said what she had to say — simply." Our talk is often laden with irony, asides, concealed forms and allusions — a mass of diplomacy and equivocation. "The Holy Virgin knew nothing of such things. She always spoke the truth — without artifice. She never kept back anything in her speech or her love. She never held back any fraction of herself or of truth . . . Like pure running water, she flowed down the slope decreed by God, moving straight and without sound, free from fear of becoming lost or soiled."

her fifth appearance bade her among other things, "If you wish to serve me, be simple, and let your actions match your words."

∞

In spiritual direction, the simple soul finds the utmost help that God has placed therein; it follows the precepts and does not abandon them, which would be weakness; but it asks for control and pays heed thereto; it does not burden one with complexities, and is ready to tell everything, without wishing to rouse interest or win approval. Here, too, it is God alone and how best to serve Him; direction, for all its usefulness, is no more than a means, to be used only to the extent to which it is useful.

To its superiors the simple soul submits readily, without any *if, but,* or *perhaps,* looking on them as the intermediaries of God's will, in the belief that no other aspect matters. Being wont to go straight for essentials, the simple soul does not pause to look for justification, and still less for excuses. Moreover, if it sees that circumstances demand some modification of plan, it takes heed of it; if it seems impossible, it consults God, and acts as well as it can in the circumstances. If it is reproved, it is not embittered, and accepts the reproof gratefully in the hope of benefitting by its experience and the lesson it has received.

With its equals the simple soul is cordial, natural, spontaneous, free from timidity or false modesty, edifying without striving to that end, and full of ardor. It is all these things because it is thinking not of itself, but of others. It guesses what will give pleasure; it knows how to handle anyone so that he will expand; it tries to get others esteemed; it is unobtrusive or active according to need — the latter never through a wish to push itself forward, but rather for the sake of guiding or instructing others. It does so, too, without apparent effort, studied effect, awkwardness, or constraint, with none of the amiability that has been cynically called "the amiability of self-discipline" — that is to say, amiability that is a visible effort.

All this the simple soul performs smoothly and easily; its angles are rounded off to meet the unexpected twists and turns of character and circumstance. There is in it nothing of one of Le Notre's gardens, with geometric patterns laid out formally. It is nearer the wonder of an arrangement in which each flower has found its own place, where picturesque walks alternate fresh coolness with bright sunlight and every few steps bring a change of scene. It is not all elaborate, fussy, squared off, and forced; the variety and the original form of the plants have been preserved. Yet the whole speaks of freshness; there has been a minimum of pruning and no overelaboration. There is a sense of freedom, of perfect control without chilliness, of views here and there opening on limitless horizons.

Simplicity of attitude: Everything is so exactly what it should be that nothing strikes the attention violently or provokes question. There is a quiet ease of manner in any meeting.

Someone said of the Abbé Pasteau, to whom we referred earlier, that when he was on vacation from his college, his attitude toward his sisters' girlfriends or his cousins was wholly reserved, but without making anyone feel uncomfortable and without any undue consideration or withdrawing. "Being used to living with his sisters and cousins, the Abbé was not afraid of feminine influences." Probably these girls, too, possessed the same modesty and simplicity. Guy de Larigaudie, with his usual freshness and strength, gives the conditions for such uncomplicated relationships between young people in his *Etoiles au grand large:*[50] "A

[50] Ed. de l'Abeille, Lyons, 30.

warped education has only too often taught men to look on women only as an opportunity for sinning, instead of seeing them as a source of richness. Companionship between girls and boys is an infinitely lovely thing. If the girls know how to act wisely in it — and the attitude of the boys toward them depends entirely on them — they can wield an immense influence." He finishes with this prayer: "O God, grant that our sisters, the young girls, may be sound and clear in spirit, to be the purity and grace in our rough lives; that they may be simple with us, kind as mothers, without deceit or affectation. Let no evil come between us; but may we, both boys and girls, be for each other a source, not of trespass, but of spiritual richness."

Another of the same type, Pierre Gaudillière, met "a friendly group of young men and women" in the university city, when he was a student. Speaking of these girls, he says, "That was a discovery for me of how much women matter to us in regard to delicacy, modesty, and kindness," adding rather charmingly, "or rather, not a discovery, after having watched my mother for so long, but a deepening, an extension from the family to the social sphere."[51]

Let us remember the well-known saying, "To the pure all things are pure." Those who are truly simple will form the right judgment on all things and on everyone.

The Abbé Long-Hasselmans may be quoted as a kindred spirit of the Abbé Pasteau; he, too, was only a student when he decided to dedicate himself to God. The nearer he came to accomplishing this, the deeper he became, the purer, and the more detached. "I am become broader in outlook," he notes one day. "Love is good in essence. Let there be no more prudery. If only the attitude be

---

[51] *Pierre Gaudillière*, notes collected by his father (Arthaud, Grenoble), 237.

simple and near to God." His biographer adds, "His outlook was becoming simple. He was seeing further because he was looking higher, more truly because he was looking straighter."[52]

Surely it was in the same sense that Louis Gillet was able to say of Fra Angelico, whose women are so pure, so ethereal, so far remote from any sensuality, "His purity of heart saved any need for anxiety: nature was without tricks for him, for his very simplicity defeated any attempted trickery. Being free from all selfish desires, he could rejoice in any creation as a masterpiece of the Supreme Artist."[53] Under this exaggerated phrasing — for no one on this earth is confirmed in grace — one can see what the writer meant: simplicity carried to its ultimate ideal almost performs the miracle of removing the very temptation to sin.

∞

In the performance of good works, the simple soul instinctively achieves two things: a complete faithfulness in devoting itself to helping its neighbor, without personal interest or suspicion of vanity; and a deliberate sobriety in the choice of such works, at least when it has a free choice. The simple soul avoids overburdening itself, knowing that feverish activity does not produce good; for here again, multiplicity can bring nothing but harm — not only to the soul itself, but also to its neighbor.

We have already quoted the Abbé Pasteau. Here is another excerpt. He considers his role as a priest in the Army and its results very little, judged by the visible effect on the troops, and understandably a source of sorrow to him. Then, continuing his reflection, he writes, "The true essence of priesthood does not lie in

---

[52] Ludovic Giraud (Ed. Publiroc, Marseilles), 45.

[53] *Histoire artistique des Ordres mendiants* (Flammarion), 188.

ceremony or even in prayer, but simply in making this offering and this sacrifice in the name of all, in the name of those who make them without knowing or understanding . . . A complete deliverance, clear beyond description . . ."

To be sure, a chaplain is not a Carthusian and would be failing in his task if he neglected the work entrusted to him. Yet his care of souls is only of secondary value, the prime fact being the action on physical matter of Jesus Christ in the Mass.[54] It often happens that so much thought is given to the soul that God is neglected. It is this error that Rémy Pasteau attempts to refute, almost brusquely; for himself, Providence had severed him from his "temptation." He writes, "My role as priest in this life where I have no real ministry is now no more than this one essential act — instead of all the varied distraction of the apostolate. I offer, consecrate and suddenly change, by my priesthood, my outward uselessness to that which is still lacking in Christ's suffering to bring about His kingdom."

One can understand what he means by the "distractions of the apostolate." Properly understood, the phrase applies to only too many cases. We urge good works: ought we not rather to urge exteriorization to avoid forgetting the real essential? The unity of *contemplata aliis tradere* has been lost, for we have forgotten the essential — *contemplata*.

Laymen indulging in good works are equally in danger from multiplicity. Surrounded by so many who do nothing, those who wish to accomplish something in that direction often display a feverish zeal — too many works, too much haste, or excessive anxiety to succeed in them, however devout their intention.

---

[54] St. Thomas Aquinas is formal: the priest has a double role: "*Unum principalem, supra Corpus Christi verum: alterum sectindarium, supra Corpus mysticum*" (*Summa Theologica*, Suppl., Q. 36, art. 2).

Not that enthusiasm is a bad thing; one can never have too much of it — never even enough. But true enthusiasm is combined with a wise inner calm. In too many forms of proselytism prayer is lacking; and therein lies the reason for the fruitlessness of so many apostolates.[55] Better to reduce the extent and to work deeper, to cover less ground and come nearer the source of true fecundity.

[55] Pope Pius XII, when Msgr. Théas flew to visit him in December 1944, bade the gallant Bishop of Montauban to preach it far and wide. The *Documentation catholique* of December 24, 1944, gives the text.

Chapter 5

∞

The Soul's Relationship with Itself

We have already noted that simplicity, being a primary idea, can be defined only by its contrasts: what is not complex is simple. The trouble is that such "complexities" are beyond numeration, ranging from what is properly called duplicity, deliberate hypocrisy, and unconscious deception, to versatility, rapid changing of ideas, vacillation, ill-defined theorizing, continual doubt, the lack of harmony between principles and practice, affectation, a sense of complication, scruples of conscience — to give only a few forms of "plurality."

Here we are concerned only with such of our complexities as affect our relationship with ourselves; even of these there is a whole host. It has indeed been suggested that the "highest comedy played by man is within himself."

∞

There is one sort of self-deception that is comparatively simple and on which we need not dwell. The cartoonist Gavarni, as a young man, was put to work in an architect's office. The Goncourts describe how, when he grew bored with copying plans, he used to spin his compasses: if they finished up pointing toward the street, he would give himself time off; if they finished pointing in some other direction, he simply started spinning again, in the hope they would finish up as he wished.

A list of similar cases could be prolonged indefinitely and be instructive enough; but as a general rule, the lack of simplicity takes a less straightforward form in a certain lack of absolute directness of intention.

"With two wings a man is lifted up above earthly things: that is with simplicity and purity," says the author of the *Imitation*. "Simplicity must be in the intention, purity in the affection."[56]

Almost the same idea was expressed by St. Francis de Sales: "Simplicity is like water: the best is the clearest, least compounded, and purest . . . Sweet Simplicity is the daughter of Innocence and the sister of Charity."

Omitting Charity, with which we are not at the moment concerned, we will reserve our consideration for purity of intention.

"What road must we follow to appear before God?" asks Ruysbroeck. "The road of most perfect likeness to Him . . . Simplicity of intention gathers into the unity of the spirit the scattered forces of the soul and unites the spirit itself with God; traversing and penetrating all places, all created things, it finds God in His profundity." The learned Fleming continues, "In every possible action we must retain, use, and develop simplicity above all things. Full of faith in God and faithful to Him, it embraces hope and charity . . . It is simplicity that will win for me the inheritance prepared for me by eternity."[57]

If, as we have seen above, the chief characteristic of God's perfection is simplicity, we cannot be surprised that simplicity should

---

[56] Thomas à Kempis, *Imitation of Christ*, Bk. 2, ch. 4, no. 1.

[57] From *L'ornement des Noces Spirituelles* in E. Hello, *Morceaux choisis de Rusbrock* (Perrin), 33, 38.

also play the greatest part in perfecting His thinking creation. This cannot be simple physically; but it can achieve moral simplicity, and must strive with all its strength for that achievement.

This moral simplicity consists in taking God as the only standard in one's thoughts and reasoning, as the object of all one's desires and the aim of all one's actions, in referring everything to Him and preferring His pleasure above all things. It was in this way that Job, who, the Bible tells us, was "a man simple and upright,"[58] was wont to act. The spirit is truly simple in its intention when, like a straight line, it takes the shortest way to its goal, without being twisted toward another objective or bending back on itself. It is truly simple when it achieves that ability to see only God; it attains perfect simplicity when, as Consummata[59] said of herself, it forces itself "to live in a state of perfect unity," striving for the most perfect union of heart, intention, and desire with Him who is above all and absolutely *one*, and who wishes only to draw us into His glorious Unity.

God is one in a unity possible only for Him. He is one and leads everything necessarily to His unity. He is one, and all who wish to be united with Him can achieve such union only by possessing His unity. To be holy, then, the soul must become *one* by cleaving, heart and spirit, to Him alone — for Him alone. If, at the same time it is seeking God, the soul is considering itself and separating its own interest from that of God, it is not one and is not simple morally because it has two objects in view. There is no better reason than this why there should be someplace where, after death, all the dross can be removed from the soul which in its time on earth has allowed its pure metal to be corroded, or which has not

[58] Job 1:1.

[59] Marie-Antoinette de Geuser, whom we have already mentioned.

removed by expiation every trace of complexity and multiplicity before leaving for the other life. We shall be permitted to see and to enjoy God only on the day when there is no longer in us any vestige of what had been other than Him.

Let us, then, strive still more for simplicity in the motives on which we act, expelling digression, excessive forethought, suspicion, distrust, overcareful argument, together with self-satisfaction, the pursuit of self-interest — which would not be subordinated to God's interest, and would therefore be a deviation from uprightness. We must also guard carefully against our natural inclinations, which only too often lead us astray. St. Ignatius of Loyola advised his followers, as a major point of his teaching, to seek God only in everything: *Ut in omnibus quaerant Deum.*[60]

It is surely of this purity of intention that our Lord is speaking in a text that seems hard to understand and is yet really sufficiently clear. St. Luke has preserved it for us, and it is read as the Epistle on, for instance, the feast of St. Martin on November 11: "The light of thy body is thy eye. If thy eye be single, thy whole body will be lightsome," and conversely: "But if it be evil, thy body also will be darksome" — that is to say, all will go ill: your foot will stumble; your head will be in danger, and your whole body in peril of falling. Scholars and thinkers[61] believe that our Lord was thinking of the power and control of intention either for good or for evil, intention controlling our activities in the same way that the eye guides our members and all our bodily movements. Intention is a "simple

---

[60] *Sommaire des Constitutions*, rule 17.

[61] See, for instance, Father Lagrange's *Saint Luc* (Gabalda), 340. Some commentators parallel this text and that from the Song of Songs (4:1) in which the Bridegroom, describing and praising the beauty of the Bride, begins with her eyes (that is, her intentions), and considers them the source of all goodness and perfection in her.

and clear eye" which has its effect on every one of our actions, even the indefinite, and makes them precious before God. An eye troubled or afflicted by grit is ill intention, which darkens all our works and makes of them works of darkness, or at least renders them of less service to the glory of God.

So we must be on our guard — I will not say against evil intention, which is a subject in itself and outside the scope of our present inquiry, but against any complexity in our intentions, against the wish to be admired, against secret self-satisfaction when we do good or when we turn to prayer and find comfort therein, against seeking contact with God for the pleasure we obtain therefrom, against being too pleased if our devotion succeeds or too troubled if it fails, to list only a few of the many possibilities.

In our daily life, we must ensure that the actions of people and things do not delay or halt us; that they do not serve as a screen to hide God from us, but rather as a pedestal to raise us to the All-Highest.

There is a story that in the days of the first monks, one ascetic stood in the doorway of his cell, holding a leaf up to the light, and gazed on it with tears running down his cheeks. Someone asked him, "Why do you weep, Father? What do you see in that leaf?" And he answered, "I see Christ crucified."

We must endeavor to discover Him who created all things in the existence and working of all created things. We must recognize secondary causes for what they are, and move straight to the prime cause: unity, simplicity, and purity of intention.

Religious writers note that it is hard to accomplish this complete purity of intention. Born complex, we have difficulty in achieving our complete release from self and in gaining complete purity. "We know very well," writes Faber, "that never, since we were born, have we ever done any one single action *entirely* for any one single motive. So that here, quite unconsciously, we may be laying claim to a very high and rare grace, to which only a few even of the canonized saints have attained."[62] Nevertheless, we must strive with all that is in us for complete rectitude and purity in the motives for our actions.

∞

Because it has a complete trust in God, the simple soul does not burden itself with irrelevant preoccupations, but thinks those that touch its immediate duty sufficient. One day should be lived at a time, for when tomorrow comes, it, too, will be called today and can then be considered. The manna fell every morning in the wilderness, and the Hebrews had enough of it throughout their sojourn there.

This does not in any way mean that the simple soul does not understand difficulties; simplicity is not oversimplification. Its faith, however, strengthens its hope. As St. Francis de Sales rather pleasantly puts it, "The lion, which is a fine-spirited animal with faith in its own courage, moves in simplicity of heart, and will go to sleep on a main road just as happily as in some hidden lair."[63] If danger comes, then it will be met with such spiritual aid as is possible — a very different matter from living presumptuously and without thought. Prayer has been observed, necessary caution exercised — very well, then, what would be the good of seeing nothing but mountains in one's path?

Because it is accustomed to being patient in itself, the simple soul can also be patient toward things, events, and circumstances, and will not be disconcerted by anything.

---

[62] *Spiritual Conferences*, 152.
[63] *Entretien*, 12.

The Soul's Relationship with Itself

St. Francis de Sales (to whom we cannot avoid continual reference in discussing simplicity)[64] writes in his letter of October 14, 1604, to Mme. de Chantal, "A soul that has become addicted to meditation, without spiritual straightness of vision, will emerge from meditation, if it is interrupted, in a state of discontent, worry, and bewilderment; while a soul that is truly free will, under similar circumstances, emerge calmly and with kindness for its interrupter" — one is reminded of Elisabeth Leseur[65] when her husband interrupted her devotions to complain of a lost collar-stud — "for it is all one in its case whether it serves God in meditation or in helping its neighbor."

The virtue of simplicity also keeps us safe from another very grave danger: self-consideration.

[64] Perhaps nobody has better expressed the extent to which St. Francis de Sales was a model of simplicity than Dom Marmion, in a talk to the Visitandines of Meaux, in 1918, when they were refugees at Maredsous in Belgium: "What was the spirit of your Founder? It is not easy to analyze because of its simplicity. It is as if one were asked, 'What is the nature of God?' When one is very near to God in prayer and in the presence of His infinite perfection, one is completely filled with it, without reckoning exactly what it really is. If, at the end, one were asked to analyze that perfection, one would be at a loss; it would be impossible to know what to say about it, because one had been in touch with an infinite and indefinable simplicity. Well, it is something very similar that we find in the spirit of our Blessed Father, 'because he was very simple'" (*Mélanges Marmion* [Desclée de Brouwer, 1938], 69).

[65] After the death of Elisabeth Leseur (1866-1914), her atheistic husband, Felix, read the spiritual diary she had written and, influenced by it, converted to Catholicism. See *The Secret Diary of Elisabeth Leseur* (Manchester, New Hampshire: Sophia Institute Press, 1996).

Holy Simplicity

Some people fail to draw a clear enough distinction between practicing a wise examination of their consciences and the harmful habit of introspection, and are so anxious to correct their faults that they spend much time — too much time — considering themselves. This struggle against self finishes, unless one is careful, in a certain interest in self. In the case of many who lack spiritual balance, this desire to cleanse oneself does not rise beyond scrupulosity, that sad stumbling-block of so many poor good intentions. The English Oratorian, Faber, has most ably condemned what he calls "self-deceit which is scrupulous." The passage is worth quoting in full:

> The older we get, the less good can we see in scruples . . . (scrupulous men) all turn out badly. Huge continents of puerile conceit are being discovered in their souls every year. They are eaten up with that unassuming assumption, which is the most wicked of all the varieties of censoriousness. Their selfish pusillanimity is intolerable. They are a pest which religious society might almost blamelessly combine to get rid of by summary extinction. Their good is all on the surface, and wears no better than the bloom on a plum. This is a form of self-deceit which Satan very much affects. It does his work as he would have it done. It perversely fixes its attention on wrong things, that is, on things which it need not particularly attend to, and it does this exclusively . . . These are tiresome men, good to try our tempers, but otherwise such as we like to know of only at a distance, as possible, probable, or actual, like the wild beasts in Africa. A man who has duties to such people is unfortunately placed in life.[66]

[66] *Spiritual Conferences*, 180-181.

Now, that passage sounds harsh. That is because, in reading it, one considers the suffering of the penitent, rather than the torment of the confessor, which is indeed no light matter. Such torment arises from the way in which some priests are moved by a false or excessive pity to listen too kindly to endless and valueless requests for explanation, approbation, and impossible definitions. One must insist on simplicity — under obedience — or one is on the rack. Too many of those who are scrupulous flatter themselves unconsciously in believing that scrupulosity is a disease, and for that reason seek sympathy and feel they are of interest. If they could be convinced that most of the time it is only stupidity, they would be far less eager to display their absurd complications.

Msgr. Gay writes of the "Holy infancy of the spirit" in self-surrender, urging it as the tomb of scrupulosity, "that great tool of Satan, which makes the soul weak and idle by making it faint-hearted, cramping and shriveling its heart by continually pressing it back on to itself and making its life dark with a thousand clouds of futile worries, vain fears, and absurd self-tormentings."[67] He adds, "Whole books have been written on the treatment of the over-scrupulous; all that is needed is to ensure that such people achieve self-surrender."

I cannot suggest any reading more useful to those prone to introspection and constant anxiety than *La Piété Confiante*, by the

---

[67] *Vie et Vertus chrétiennes*, Vol. III, *l'Abandon*, ch. 3. If another authority is needed, the verdict of St. Vincent de Paul is summed up by Msgr. Calvet in his work, *La Littérature religieuse de François de Sales à Fénelon* (Gigord), 121: "Common sense will be the great counselor of love. Thanks to it, one danger will be swept aside — that restless subtlety which drives one to hair-splitting over duties, searching that leads nowhere, and a ceaseless going back upon our acts and our intentions. All this is a wile of the Devil. Go to God in good heart, fully and simply."

Holy Simplicity

Abbé de Tourville, from which I will quote only one passage, which is vastly valuable:

> Love our Lord with simplicity: that is, with the complete conviction of your constant great inadequacy, but happy to love Him even so. Do not seek to vie with our Lord in love; you cannot but lose in such rivalry. Only act with simplicity and humility as best you can: that will be perfection.

Chapter 6

∞

The Advantages of Simplicity

We must distinguish between the advantages of simplicity for him who practices it and for those who witness that practice.

The man who practices simplicity as we have tried to describe it has every likelihood of achieving a very well-directed spiritual life, since his relationship with God springs from the attitude of a son, which is the key to the whole matter. He also possesses the best means of controlling both himself and circumstances in every situation in which this life can place him.

Let us consider those two points more fully. No one will deny that the basis for any spiritual life that is to be perfectly fair and balanced is to be found in the relation of son to father; with God set in His proper place, above everything, acting not with the power of a master, but with the loving kindness of a father claiming our love, and what the Bible calls a "holy freedom" to serve Him: "the freedom of little children." It is that above all that our Lord came to teach us: He spoke only of the Father and was concerned only with Him.[68]

---

[68] In John 14, the Father is named twenty-three times in thirty-one verses. Cf. Matt. 6:9: "When you pray, ye shall say, 'Our Father.'" The texts are numerous and the attitude beyond question.

Holy Simplicity

Before any action, He would lift up His eyes to His Father, inviting us to do the same. Dying, He delivered His soul to the Father, in the wish that we should follow His example in our last moments. The most fundamental dogma of the gospel is that God the Father adopted us in Jesus Christ, raised us in Him to the dignity of sonship, and so assured us that we should enter upon the inheritance of the Father at the appointed time. It would be easy to show that the title "children of God" implies and reminds us of the principal objects of our faith, the very foundation of our hope and the main motive for our love.

However, nothing, unfortunately, is rarer than that relationship of a son toward the Father, that holy and loving freedom of the children of God. How many there are whose fear of God is far greater than their love! How many really have enough intelligence of spirit to entrust themselves to Him, in the faith that their interests are far safer in His hands than in their own? How many there are who are quite willing to look on God as their Father so long as things go well with them, but who, if those benefits disappear, lose faith and see in Him only a harsh — or, at best, forgetful — master!

The virtue of simplicity could do much to straighten out such kinds of warping. A father is surely just as much a father when he seeks to strengthen his child as when he fondles his child. The simple soul does not consider itself, for it is free, or striving its hardest to be free, from any selfishness of outlook. It finds the ways of God excellent whatever happens. Whether or not it receives comfort, it serves and only wishes to serve, without consideration of reward, knowing that God is its Father and understands its needs. If things are painful, God the Father is there to give counsel; it is His child. If everything seems to be going contrary to its wishes, it is surely best not to wish for anything but what God wishes and ordains.

What unity, what sweetness — unearthly sweetness — and what peace lie in that!

We need not suppose that simplicity prevents us from reproaching God tenderly upon occasion; on the contrary, that holy freedom allows it.[69] He was not angry with Teresa of Avila when, overwhelmed by suffering, she said to Him, "O Lord, if this is how You treat Your friends, I can understand why You have so few!" There is in that, not a frozen reserve, but a whole code of Christianity: the opening of the heart — with the respect due to the distance, the vast distance, between the Infinite and the finite, between absolute Purity and our miserable sinning, and the holy simplicity that can overcome that distance.

As one of the greatest writers on spiritual life, Father Grou, puts it so well:

> We must leave God to rule our hearts; must yield ourselves peaceably to grace, considering His holy will in all things and setting nothing against it. We must overcome our vain reflections; calm our imaginations and disregard the alarm and fright that harm His goodness; for therein lies our path to Heaven. If there are thorns in it, we must not complain, for they are of our own sowing.

Simplicity does more than ensure that our moral conduct toward God shall be correct; it urges us to ever deeper recognition of God's claims to our love.

[69] Consider rather Abraham's prayer to God for the just men in Sodom and Gomorrah: "Far be it from Thee to do this thing, and to slay the just with the wicked . . . this is not beseeming Thee; Thou who judgest all the earth wilt not make this judgment" (Gen. 18:25). Job and some of the prophets after him did not hesitate to voice similar remonstrances, and the Almighty yields to their simplicity.

Holy Simplicity

A child likes to look at his mother; he does not find it enough not to fail in respect for her, not to disobey her or make her sad. He will look at her steadily and seem never to weary of such loving study. Such behavior would be rude from a stranger; but from him it is natural and to his credit. The simple soul behaves similarly with God. Not only does its activity, filled with His spirit, develop in the most serene trust and the purest faith, but it wishes to know more and more of the God it loves, and seeks, as if by instinct, to learn everything it can about its most Holy Father. This produces a joyful eagerness for everything that can reveal Him — the study of religious works, prayer, and meditation — through the feeling that he is God's child and in such a way that that sense of sonship may be deepened.

∞

Besides the advantages that simplicity gives to him who practices it in his relationship with God, we must mention the advantages that simplicity gives the soul in all aspects of its life on earth. It produces a magnificent confidence, which nothing can shake: it allows the soul to pass through anything without digressions or considerations of interest, rendering impotent all hasty, anxious, or ill-timed precautions.

Remember the sage who, when Athens was at her height, saw that most men were burdened with infinite possessions, seeking honors and a life of ease, and who decided that he, for his part, would dispense with everything that made for ease of living and set an example of utter simplicity. "It is the chief characteristic of the gods," said he, "that they have no wants: the less wants one has, then, the closer one will come to them." He saw one day a small boy, who had broken his plate, making a hole in his bread to hold his lentils. Exclaiming that he was beaten, that the child lived more simply than he did, the sage cast away his plate. On another occasion, he saw a child use the hollow of its hand to drink from a fountain: and, because he saw he still had something he did not need, he at once broke his own beaker.

If there was something of pride in his attitude, we may ignore it; for we have magnificent examples among Christians that are certainly full of complete humility — in Francis of Assisi, in the old hermits, and, more recently, in de Foucauld. They had complete freedom. If, then, circumstances compel us to live in the greatest simplicity, we should think of those brave souls who chose of their own free will to give up everything.

It is far harder to rid oneself of self than of some material possession, for we have always to struggle against self-esteem. We must not hesitate — and see how freely the soul moves, in joy at its liberation.

There is one type of humility which produces timidity. By urging consideration of one's own weaknesses, it saps courage — that very necessary and useful belief in oneself without which no decision, action, or choice is possible. Simplicity has solved that problem even before it arises — not through rashness or imprudence, but because instinctively, intuitively almost, it has lifted itself clear of the brambles in its way and rears its trunk, firm and unshakable, toward the open heavens. How much time has been gained, how many anxieties avoided by its directness!

To many this may come happily and easily by nature; for others it means a pure trust in God, a clarity of vision, and the practice of going straight to the heart of a problem. In most cases this virtue comes naturally or without effort; but it might sometimes be achieved only by a great struggle. In either case, how happy are they whose realm is the light and whose deepest longing is integrity!

Holy Simplicity

∞

While simplicity is precious to him who practices it, it is not less so for those who witness its practice in others. "There is a great charm in the beauty of simplicity," says St. Francis de Sales. "I would always give a hundred serpents in exchange for one dove."

We have no liking for complicated characters, with all their intricacies, who are submerged under a thousand turnings and twistings. What we like is the spirit that goes straight to an answer; a heart that will love without a constant investigation of the merits of the object of its love, or of its reason for loving. We dislike fops, the vain, and those who love to show off, who enjoy the sound of their own voice, or who try to praise themselves. It is not esteem that they win; more often it is a rebuke — as in the case of Luigi Braschi, a nephew of Pius VI. He proudly displayed his twenty coaches to the Marquis de Breteuil, the Ambassador to Malta, asking, "How do you like my hundred coaches?" and received the reply, "I like these twenty well enough; we must see the others some time." The simple soul strives to improve itself fundamentally: it hates bluff, and would willingly follow the d'Arsonval motto: *Paraître ne veux quand être je peux* ("I do not wish to *seem*, when I can *be*"). We do not like people who are over-ceremonious, with gestures too pompous or too studied. We do not admire hair too well-kept, with too perfect a parting to it; or too flowery a speech; a page too meticulously arranged. Some forms of overperfection would really be more perfect if they contained some imperfection, as evidence of naturalness, instead of so much obvious striving after absolute correctness. We really ask a little less constraint, a little more evidence that, even if better than we are, you are still like us!

It is with reason that the Church does not as a rule canonize those whose holiness suggests too much striving. She prefers a pleasant ripeness, rounded and well developed, which is indeed based on renunciation — but on a renunciation whose outer roughnesses have been softened by love to such an extent that something supernatural has become something almost natural; in the same way that the rough threads in velvet, for all their solidity, cannot be seen, and one can forget its maker's efforts as one looks at it.

It is not just dislike, but detestation that one feels for duplicity. It does little enough to aid the reputation of Anatole France when we learn of an incident recounted by Armory in his *Cinquante ans de Vie Parisienne*. He entertained the "Comrades" who came to the Villa Saïd to pay respect to the great "democratic" writer — and, as soon as his guests had left, he had the room aired and perfumed, and changed into a smart lounge-suit.

Another who posed as a friend of the common people was Sébastien Faure, who was not above passing time in smart society. Once, one of his acquaintances met him at an evening party. There he was — no longer the tribune of the people, in a peaked cap — smartly dressed, with a white tie and polished shoes — and very mortified at being seen so well turned out, begging his friend never to let the workers who attended his public harangues know of this bourgeois side of his life.

In another sphere, does it enhance our regard for Renan if we know that his skepticism allowed him to make such a volte-face as he made with the Hellenistic scholar Ménard? The latter requested the great man to write a preface to his book on Hermes Trismegistos. That preface began, "It is an easier matter to show how doctrines end up than to tell how they began." When Ménard interrupted, questioning this, Renan hurriedly changed it to, "It is *not* . . ." The manuscript with the alteration is still extant.

Surely one of the main reasons for our Lord's condemnation of the worldly spirit is that the world approves of this double-dealing, giving more importance to what shows outwardly than to reality, allowing a pretense to be what one is not, the creation of an illusion of virtue or, at least, of integrity; while at the same time barring no scheming, compromise, or machination that will help one to "get there." The Master condemned the Pharisees in a phrase that will live forever: "whited sepulchers."[70]

I do not mean that it is wrong to be clever; one can be clever and still be simple. I would rather say that simplicity is the best sort of cleverness. There is instinctive distrust the moment there is any suspicion of scheming, of complicated planning or maneuvering below the surface, of "I give you this to gain that," or "I tell you this to get you to tell me that." Contrast that with the attraction of St. Paul's straightforwardness as he writes to the Corinthians:

> Our glory is this: the testimony of our conscience, that in simplicity of heart and sincerity of God, and not in carnal wisdom, but in the grace of God, we have conversed in this world; and more abundantly toward you. For we write no other things to you than what you have read and known.[71]

During the political campaign against the religious congregations in France, the man most feared by the enemies of the Church was M. Grousseau, a thin little wisp of a man, but absolutely upright, simple in his speech, and with a purity of heart that gave him singular moral greatness. He was no demagogue; he spoke without any subtlety. But when he spoke in the Chamber, it was as if a ray of light had entered a darkened place, a ray coming straight from the sun to strike men's spirits. It would have won men's hearts had they not been impenetrably encircled in triple steel. One

[70] Matt. 23:27.
[71] 2 Cor. 1:12-13.

might withhold one's vote; one could not withhold one's assent and admiration.

It may be asked if the practice of such honesty does not involve us in the danger of being taken in the snares of those who are accustomed to employing deceit and veiled hypocrisy. Yet did not our Lord, when He sent us out like sheep into the midst of wolves, bidding us "be simple as doves," also warn us to be "wise as serpents"?[72] While, then, honesty undisguised will often be the height of wisdom, we are not forbidden to take precautions, to find out with whom we have to deal or to ascertain our neighbor's character. What simplicity avoids is previous condemnation of others' actions, an uncharitable or suspicious interpretation of their intentions — the *a priori* doubt that St. Thomas Aquinas justly rebukes: "It is better to make many mistakes, and to hurt no one, than to run the risk of thinking ill of someone who does not deserve it."

[72] Matt. 10:16.

Chapter 7

∞

A Difficult but Desirable Virtue

There is a passage in one of our modern novels in which a young woman asks her father, an eminent professor of philosophy, "Father, has your philosophy ever been of any use to you in your life?"

"Why, of course, my dear; it got me my job."

"And that was all?"

"All? Surely that is enough?"

"I mean has your philosophy ever been of use to you in the serious things of life?"

Her worthy father has to admit that it has not; and he suggests a moment later, "One has to become as a little child"; adding with a smile, "That is not easy for a university professor."

We will omit consideration of philosophy as taught and understood by some — which does not concern us here[73] — and note only the final phrase, "one has to become as a little child." We can admit that such simplicity, with its renunciation of all spiritual

[73] The belief in simplicity is really the revelation of the gospel. Philosophy already could give a man considerable aid in becoming simple — if it were studied as a science of life rather than an account of systems.

pride, is no easy matter for a professor. Simplicity in any sense is not easy for anyone.

Father Faber, who described it in its widest sense of Christian sincerity, said that it consisted of three things: honesty with oneself; honesty with others; and honesty with God — and, he adds, "any one of those three things is rarer than the Australian black swan."

∞

Here are three reasons simplicity is difficult for us. In the first place, we are complex by nature. In the second, our way of life is artificial and complicated. In the third, our spiritual education often fails to develop openness and breadth, and tends more toward involution than to free and joyous expansion.

We are composed by nature of body and soul, matter and spirit. So, being born mixed, we always have great difficulty in escaping that complexity. We find it easier to be compound than to be simple; alongside noble impulses we find very worldly desires. How fortunate are the angels in being pure spirit, while we are spirits imbedded in stuff so different from spirit! We have within us the stuff of which angels are made; all the same, we are warned that we cannot be angels all the time. Even without outside guidance, something within us warns us that what Pascal calls "the beast" is not far away. Not the "beast" in the sense of some savage and lustful gorilla, but simply meaning the animal outlook with its selfishness and self-interest — so far removed from the aspirations of the seraphim and the archangels.

We are not only a "mixture"; we are also a battlefield. Over and above this duality of matter and spirit, we must consider, as we had to consider earlier, the fact so dramatically inscribed in our very core: Original Sin and its tragic result, evil desire. Our spirit, which left God's hands so lovely a thing, above and outside nature, revolted against God. In other words, it was not intended that we should be just human. God had allowed us to share His own life, and, so that this divine life might be the better rooted in us and adapted to our life more pleasantly, He had freed us, not only from death and from suffering, but also from the inner struggle between the powers of good and the powers of evil. In this perfect harmony, the faculties we call inferior — imagination and sensibility — obeyed without question the higher faculties of pure reason illuminated by grace. Then man disobeyed God. In consequence, man is no longer master within himself. Imagination and sensibility strive to conquer reason, in an almost continual struggle. Even if man managed to master everything else, he would still have to master himself. In the words of Jacques Rivière, "Myself I shall have always with me."

Some natures are cooler, better balanced, less passionate; and at every step God is present with His mercy. But one can imagine the effort that is necessary for one without special gifts to live always in complete uprightness, free from vain fears, thinking the best of his neighbor's actions, placing his whole faith in God, without judging or allowing himself to be influenced by people or events; for one who seeks to enclose himself in what is a freedom, not a restriction — the saying of a perpetual "Amen. So it is; so be it. All is well. Let our Lord be glorified. Nothing else matters to me."

∞

The second reason simplicity is difficult for us is that all around us we find artificiality, complications, and conventions.

In youth the candor of the child survives for a longer or shorter time in relation to the conditions of his upbringing. There is a gradual adaptation to his environment. He hears the maid say,

Holy Simplicity

"Madam is not at home," when he is quite certain his mother *is* in. He hears criticism of a visitor who has just left; yet only just before, while talking to that same visitor, Father and Mother were as sweet as they could be. At school, we find our companions cheating and cribbing, asking us the meaning of a word or the answer to a problem, and looking on those who will not join in this as bad sports. At the university, film fans bribe the porter to let them in at midnight or one o'clock in the morning after going to the cinema on nights when it is forbidden, scamping their work, or pretending to be taking notes in lectures when they are really drawing or writing letters.

Now, those are only a few examples out of a host. How, then, could they live, when they are grown up, other than as they lived while their characters were forming? The habit is there — and the temptations are greater. Even when there are no great faults, what has been lost irretrievably, but for a few exceptions through God's mercy, is the complete uprightness, the absolute candor, and the loyalty that are the pure virginity of simplicity.

Even where there is no moral failing, there is still room for things opposed to simplicity. Consider snobbery and the eccentricities it produces, the slavery it can engender, and the gradings to which it can give birth. Consider the ways of public gatherings, where all is false, display and dust in the eyes — artificial setting; artificial souls; artificial talk. Listen to an academic discourse or a public toast — things to be shunned. Such a burning of incense, with nobody believing a word of what is said — simply a necessary sacrifice to convention!

The language of some Churchmen is not wholly free from this evil convention. Take away from many formal sermons, marriage addresses, and speeches all bombast, ornament, and "style" — and what would be left? Let us stick to facts and omit these superfluous or obsolete panegyrics. X, Y, or Z may have acted devoutly; nothing could be better, but spare the incense. Did they act for God or for the world? Let God reward them. Leave out those pompous adjectives, those vain family trees, those high-flown phrases. If such be necessary for information, well and good; but do not wrap it up in a ton of what Huysmans would have called "holy grease." We have no time to lose: the house is on fire. We must be direct, vigorous if it be in us — and always clear, ridding ourselves once and for all of this manner of speaking, so deplorably "unnatural," which has lasted far too long.[74]

The world is building itself afresh; let us find once more the undying novelty of simplicity. It is not a matter of barring wise customs or politeness (which is unfortunately only too often forgotten), but of preventing oneself from becoming artificial. If every man examines himself, it will be much.

It must be admitted that a certain stamp of soul is necessary if one is to resist one's environment; even those who try to struggle against it usually allow themselves sooner or later to be submerged, and come down to the general level. One writer puts it, "Most of those capable of independent thought soon leave the stage where compromise is abhorrent and come, at first with dislike and soon with satisfaction, to accept a code of worldly conventions that Steele described as 'a method of making the wise and the fools equal.' "[75]

---

[74] In a slightly different sense — but one still related to our theme — was an address given to his clergy at New Year 1945 by the Archbishop of Toulouse, Msgr. Saliège. In this he said, with his usual frankness, "In the first place, we do not know how to speak. If we are to be understood, people must know our language. We speak a language that is foreign to them, using words that are no longer in current use. In short, ecclesiastical language is not understood any more. We must shed it."

[75] Gissing, *Né en exil* (Ed. du Siècle), 244.

Holy Simplicity

In the period before the War, there were here and there some signs of a struggle for a return to simplicity of living. There was a wish to shake off the artificial restriction of luxury and comfort and sophisticated pleasure, and to praise a return to the fresh air, the open road, and a healthy life. The Scout movement has had a great influence in this direction. That offers an excellent method of recapturing the spirit of the simple life through a feeling of sacrificing comfort and idleness. Other movements, too, worked in the same direction in different ways, and are to be congratulated on it.

Then came the vast catastrophe; the crash of armies; evacuations; shelling; bombing; life in prison, in camps, or at forced labor; restrictions and civil strife. Every man had to cut down his style of living, to simplify his life; the pressure of events subdued the most rebellious spirits. "There is no greater simplifying force than a disaster."[76] That is true enough. And this was a disaster on so vast a scale; let us at least retain from it the taste for simplicity.

∞

There is a third reason simplicity is comparatively scarce that has especial value for some of the devout.

The Acts of the Apostles tells us that the first Christians served God *cum exaltatione et simplicitate cordis* — "with gladness and simplicity of heart."[77] They had found God, and so possessed the real formula for a true life: the riches of the supernatural opened unbounded before them, an incomparable solace in the midst of our sufferings in the low vale of life. For them all was Heaven: here below, a Heaven of mercy; above, a Heaven of glory; because God in

---

[76] Thibon, *Retour au réel*, 179.
[77] Acts 2:46.

A Difficult but Desirable Virtue

His holiness possessed every moment. Charity ruled all of them. Men said, "See how they love one another!" They exhorted one another to be pure as their baptism demanded, to be patient under the threat of martyrdom; and, if they had to die for their faith, *ibant gaudentes* — they went with joy in their hearts. It would never have occurred to them to look on the service of their Lord as something complicated or made up of manifold observances; they went straight to God, to their brothers, to the procurator, to Heaven.

No doubt they possessed special blessings — what we may call "initial blessings." The spirit was supreme; and, as for the letter, which was not always defined or the same in every community, one simply did as well as one could. Later, understandably, rules became fixed; not as an addition to dogma, but from the necessity of adapting the spiritual way of life to different souls. When there is a crowd, one must perforce lower the level that can be attained by a select few. Any increase in quantity brings a risk of a lowering of quality. Many of the faithful became mediocre, were satisfied with a Christianity with the brakes on; some twistings of the divine law were looked on in some places as the inevitable result of human frailty. It is understandable that, from that time, the leaders should lay increasing stress on wrongdoing, the struggle against sin, and the control of the senses. In the beginning there was a thirst to serve God as well as possible; men's souls were swept along by enthusiasm, and it was less a matter of guarding against cowardice than controlling their ardor. Then came a time when it was necessary to arouse courage, to fix at least a minimum level below which they could not go without committing a supplementary fault. Just recall that a special order was needed to make the baptized receive their Lord at least once a year in the Eucharist!

It was no longer a matter of addressing the bulk of Christians as if they longed to remain fervent; it was that they made so little effort in that direction. Stress was placed on the formidable: salvation, death, Hell, temptation. Men were urged to consider their souls. In order that they might remain steadfast in the midst of worldly things, it was necessary to suggest aids by increasing outward ceremony. Eager souls, who had less need for such rules, took for themselves what had been aimed at the majority. Some misunderstood; many fell from examination of conscience, which is an excellent thing when practiced intelligently and held within fixed limits, into the habit of introspection. Here and there, scrupulosity became rife — a triumph of absurd and lamentable complication, which we have already discussed. Many, even those who were otherwise well balanced and generous, lived under the rule of fear rather than love. So it created almost a revolution in the ranks of the godly when St. Thérèse of the Child Jesus spread the doctrine of the spirit of liberal trust, which she called her "Little Way" and which was to be the grand triumphal way for all the friends of God.

This is no matter of praising an easy Christianity, shorn of spiritual effort, but of giving or restoring to Christians the true spirit of the gospel — a spirit of peace, of self-surrender, of freedom from the mechanical and from all tangles of unnecessary complication.

If we wish Christianity to appear to all as what it really is, as something splendidly attractive, especially if we wish it to appear to the masses — who hate artificiality and complication — as a message from on high, and that it should draw to itself souls who have fallen away, it is supremely important that we should show a clean outline. It must be a piece of architecture whose lines climb high into the sky, unencumbered by superfluous construction — a cathedral with a fine tower unspoiled by useless embellishments to mark the taste of one age or by the arbitrary patching of workmen of another.

In dealing with subtler souls, we must take care that a mass of complicated explanation does not make them forget the sweet purity of true spirituality. Thinking, no doubt, of St. Paul's *Simplices filii Dei*,[78] Msgr. de Segur wrote, "Nothing is so simple as (true) piety and the inner life. It is very simple because it is divine; and the saints are only perfectly simple sons of God."

Of this we can be sure: a man possesses a very fully developed virtue when he can practice with supernatural perfection toward God, toward his neighbor, and toward himself the most perfect simplicity. The fact that simplicity is a difficult virtue does not prevent it from being a very desirable one. The Bible is our first evidence for that.

The first verse of the book of Wisdom exhorts us, "Seek God in simplicity of heart" — that is, in all uprightness and sincerity. If we read through Ecclesiasticus[79] we find praise for one or another form of simplicity at every step.

"Be not a hypocrite in the sight of men,
and let not thy lips be a stumbling-block to thee."[80]

"Woe to them that are of a double heart . . .
and have gone aside into crooked ways."[81]

"Justify not thyself before God,
for He knoweth the heart; and
desire not to appear wise before the King."[82]

---

[78] "Sincere children of God" (Phil. 2:5).

[79] RSV = Sirach.

[80] Ecclus. 1:37 (RSV = Sir. 1:29).

[81] Ecclus. 2:14, 16 (RSV = Sir. 2:12).

[82] Ecclus. 7:5 (RSV = Sir. 7:5).

> "My son, meddle not with many matters . . .
> for if thou pursue after, thou shalt not overtake."[83]

> "Young man, scarcely speak in thy own cause.
> If thou be asked twice, let thy answer be short.
> In many things be as if thou wert ignorant;
> and hear in silence and withal seeking."[84]

The Book of Proverbs, too, shows many more or less direct references to simplicity.

> "His communication is with the simple"[85] (He reveals
> Himself to little ones, and according to the sense
> of the Hebrew text, discloses His secrets to them).

> "The path of the just, as a shining light, goeth
> forward and increaseth even to perfect day."[86]

> "Remove from thee a froward mouth . . .
> make straight the path for thy feet . . .
> decline not to the right hand nor to the left."[87]

> "Justice keepeth the way of the innocent,
> but wickedness overthroweth the sinner."[88]

> "Lying lips are an abomination to the Lord;
> but they that deal faithfully please Him."[89]

---

[83] Ecclus. 11:10 (RSV = Sir. 11:10).

[84] Ecclus. 32:10-12 (RSV = Sir. 32:7-9).

[85] Prov. 3:32.

[86] Prov. 4:18.

[87] Prov. 4:24-27.

[88] Prov. 13:6.

[89] Prov. 12:22.

"A cautious man concealeth knowledge;
and the heart of fools publisheth folly."[90]

"He that keepeth his mouth keepeth his soul;
but he that hath no guard on his speech shall meet
with evils . . . The just shall hate a lying word."[91]

These few verses are enough. The New Testament is certainly not behindhand in this. Indeed, the New Testament is wholly a hymn to simplicity. In the Epistles we hear St. Paul bid us to give alms with a simple heart,[92] to serve God with a simple heart,[93] to exercise authority with a simple heart,[94] to obey with a simple heart: *Obedite . . . in simplicitate cordis, sicut Christo: Obedite in simplicitate cordis timentes Deum.*[95]

He advises the Philippians to live as "sincere children of God . . . in the midst of a crooked and perverse generation; among whom you shine as lights in the world."[96] St. James, too, urges us to approach God without fear or turning aside, in simplicity of heart and avoidance of a double mind.[97]

The purely human wisdom of the Moralists would serve as confirmation of these inspired texts, if such confirmation were necessary.

---

[90] Prov. 12:23.
[91] Prov. 13:3-5.
[92] 2 Cor. 9:11-13.
[93] 2 Cor. 11:3.
[94] Rom. 12:8.
[95] Eph. 6:5; Col. 3:22.
[96] Phil. 2:15.
[97] James 1:6-7; 4:8.

Holy Simplicity

Montaigne is right in noting, "In the sphere of human relations, I have often noticed that silence and modesty are two qualities that aid converse." Men should not push themselves forward; should make themselves liked without seeking to be held in honor; should, while possessing merit, refrain from flaunting it — and still more from exaggerating it. They should endeavor to love naturalness and truth, without elaboration or ostentation, and should nevertheless offer the joy of discovering in them, despite the screen of obscurity with which they veil themselves, the wealth of charm they contain. Such men Joubert describes as "so necessary to the adornment of the world and to the honor of humanity that those ages when no nation can boast of owning a number of them will be ages of barbarism."

Indeed, the best and pleasantest relationship between men springs from complete straightforwardness, prudent modesty, and pleasing simplicity. Austen Chamberlain tells the following story:[98] In about 1885, after coming down from Cambridge, he was in Paris to study politics, economics, and diplomacy. During his time there, he attended an evening function at which Anatole Leroy-Beaulieu, whose lectures he was attending, happened to be present. He took his courage in both hands, and said, "Monsieur, I have the honor to be attending your lectures, and count it a very great privilege to meet you." He was amazed to hear the eminent professor, who was as simple in private life as he was brilliant in his work, reply in a tone of perfect sincerity, "Then, sir, I am greatly in need of your indulgence." This was no mere form of politeness; still less was it humility, as we say, "fishing."

Yet here is evidence worth far more than that of even the wisest philosophers. In the beatification and canonization of our little

[98] In his memoirs, *The Thread of the Years*, 12.

St. Thérèse of the Child Jesus, Popes Benedict XV and Pius XI praised greatly the simplicity of the Carmelite of Lisieux. Pius XI said, on March 18, 1925, that everyone could and should follow the example of saintliness set by this completely simple child. This does not mean that everyone should become a Carmelite, but that everyone should build into his life that spirit of trust, of love, of willing self-surrender, and of zeal increased by little things, of which we spoke only a few pages back. And Benedict XV spoke in the same spirit of the child's way of life — understanding it so well — saying he saw in it "the secret of holiness for *all* the faithful."

The fact that some have misjudged the childlike way of living, finding in it nothing but mere sweetness or childish art, proves only that they have judged things amiss. Our little — our *great* St. Thérèse has shown many through her example and her teaching what the freedom of the child of God meant. She stands as a delightful and comparatively approachable example, in the midst of our modern complexities, of simplicity in its strongest and most attractive form.

Conclusion

How Can We Achieve Simplicity?

The very wording of the question "How can we achieve simplicity" sets a delicate problem; for it will be said that simplicity cannot be "achieved": it is possessed naturally — and technical formula will not work.

Indeed, simplicity presupposes innate qualities, a natural inclination. He who lacks this first essential will never achieve it by any formal apprenticeship and hard work. Some people, being born complex, will never be able to rid themselves completely of the love of complication. They may become godly, but their supreme virtue will never be simplicity. There will be in them a lack of spiritual balance, of considerable judgment, of calm in ordering their impressions, of control of imagination, even of health. This is sometimes due to a faulty spiritual education and a vagueness of guidance at the start of their progress, an over-great faith in the multiplicity of some material methods of sanctification or devotion.

We do not say that such souls should make no effort to become more simple, but that they will not often become real exponents of simplicity. There are many roads that lead to God. Everyone is not equally qualified to take the main road — which is no line drawn on moving earth, but flight into the clear air, without need of contact with the obstacles of earth.

If all cannot aspire to the rare simplicity that we see more or less perfect in such as Thérèse of the Child Jesus, Larigaudie, Pasteau, or Mireille Dupouey, in what direction can those who feel the desire to practice this virtue try to advance? It can really be answered by what we have already written: a brief resume should be enough.

Place God first: that is the best way of ensuring that God will one day control everything — that control being simplicity in its purest form. "Man is complex because he tries to serve two masters."

Strive in everything to see nothing but God; to wish for nothing but God.

Bring everything to God in your prayers, rejoicing in His divine fatherhood, and striving to exclude self from your devotion. You must already have worked hard enough to know yourselves; now it is a matter of striving to forget oneself.

Words are very difficult; even the phrase "working to forget oneself" may suggest a division into two — dualism. Consider carefully. There is one sort of dualism that is opposed to simplicity, because one is still concerned with oneself, even in attempting to leave oneself; and there is another division into two, performed for the remedying of some definite fault and for achieving the suppression of self.

When, for instance, we learn from the Gospel that our Lord, in performing any action, used to lift His eyes to Heaven, it is not duality. It is, on the contrary, a new reduction to oneness, which the Master Himself did not need, but which He wished to offer us as example.

In daily life, try to look at everything from God's angle. Let the spirit behind your flesh and blood control action, in uprightness of reason and purity of faith.

How Can We Achieve Simplicity?

In dealings with your neighbor, try to gain so profound an insight that you see God in others. Preachings and works of mercy are then only a prolonged contact with the inner Guest — the revelation in public of what one is in the sanctuary of one's soul. Guard against any effort to gain esteem, to win sympathy or to desire success for its own sake. Let not your left hand know what your right has given. If it is a matter of doing good, then see that the effort be simple rather than complex.

In oneself, there must be a very wide sense of duty, without endeavoring to do over-well — which suggests an element of feverish striving. Assuming you make a normal moral effort, entrust yourself to Providence. Remain true to yourself whatever happens. *Linea recta* — the straight line — always.

Raoul Plus
(1882–1958)

Raoul Plus was born in Boulogne-sur-Mer, France, where he attended the Jesuit college. In 1899 he entered the Jesuit novitiate in Amiens and was ordained there. Because of laws that persecuted religious orders at that time, Fr. Plus had to leave France in 1901 and did not return from this exile for ten years, during which time he studied literature, philosophy, and theology in Belgium and Holland. He also taught courses in the field of humanities.

At the advent of World War I, Fr. Plus enlisted as a soldier, and subsequently as chaplain, and later was awarded the *Croix de Guerre* and the *Medaille Militaire* for his heroism. It was during this time that he began to write, producing his first two books, which were followed by a host of works on various aspects of the spiritual life, and in particular, about the presence of Christ in the soul.

After the war, Fr. Plus taught religion at the Catholic Institute of Arts and Sciences in Lille and became a well-loved spiritual director for the students. During school vacations, he gave retreats for priests and seminarians and wrote several books about priests.

In his lifetime, Fr. Plus wrote more than forty books aimed at helping Catholics understand God's loving relationship with the soul. His words consistently stress the vital role of prayer in the spiritual life and seek to show how to live out important spiritual truths. His direct, practical style renders his works invaluable for those seeking to know Christ better and to develop a closer union with Him in their souls.